A FOCUSED FAITH

A FOCUSED FAITH

The songs, psalms, and reflections of

Janet S. Williams

WestBow
PRESS
A DIVISION OF THOMAS NELSON

WestBow Press books may be ordered through booksellers or by contacting:

WestBow Press
A Division of Thomas Nelson
1663 Liberty Drive
Bloomington, IN 47403
www.westbowpress.com
1-(866) 928-1240

ISBN: 978-1-4497-0869-6 (sc)
ISBN: 978-1-4497-0870-2 (dj)
ISBN: 978-1-4497-0868-9 (e)

Library of Congress Control Number: 2010941204

Printed in the United States of America

WestBow Press rev. date: 11/20/2010

For the glory of the Lord God Almighty, who was and is and is to come.

For the most precious blessing of my life, my family: my husband and best friend, Al; our son Markham and our daughter-in-law, Louise; our sons, Daniel and Jacob; our daughter, Kristine, and her son, Christopher; our granddaughters, Melissa, Stephanie, Linz, and Kate; and our great-grandsons, Josiah and Edward.

A special thank you to Pastor Eddie and Sandi B., Pastor Frank and Tippy Dennisson, and Pastor Don and Karen DuBerry for their faithfulness to Christ, which has impacted my life in such a powerful way.

Thank you to my sisters in Christ, Chickadee, Ellin, Doobie, Susan, and Sylvia, for believing in me all these years.

God bless my faithful editors, Eva J. Olson, Susan Mullins, Sandi B, and Westbow Press's excellent editorial staff.

A very special thank you to our step - daughter, Julie Montiel, owner of The Perfect Look Salon, for making me look "perfect" for my photo session.

Jesus, my Lord, it is my prayer that Your love and compassion may be seen in me and that my life may bring glory to You.

Janet S. Williams

Contents

Dear reader,

I have included my personal thoughts at the beginning of each chapter.

—Janet S. Williams

Foreword

Pastor Eddie and Sandi B.

Over two years ago, Jan joined up with Conviction for Christ Ministry. The main focus of our ministry is reaching those lost behind prison walls. This year we will share the gospel of Jesus Christ in about six hundred Bible studies throughout the United States. So often people come and go when it comes to working with those forgotten souls in prisons, but Jan has been such an asset to our work with the youth facility. Her spiritual maturity, biblical knowledge, and dependability are so important to those teens who have very few people they can count on the. What an honor and privilege it is to unveil this book to you the reader.

This book is a beautiful tapestry of stories, songs, poems, and prayers. It is perfect to read, whether your day is happy or disappointing. It crosses age barriers, being accessible to readers both young and old. The inspiration is for everyone. Whether you're a soldier in the military, a prisoner behind bars, a wife, a mother, married, single, or a grieving soul, there is a surprise inside this book for you.

In life, sometimes it is hard to express what you're feeling inside. Jan's gift to write her life experiences of both joy and pain will give you the right words your heart is looking for. As Jan has warmed the hearts of so many teens behind the prison walls who have experienced so much pain and hurt in their lives, I know the words in this book have been given by God to touch your heart and give you *A Focused Faith*. So get started, and focus on what God has for you through the pages of this book.

Pastor Eddie and Sandi B.
Founders of Conviction for Christ Ministry
P.O. Box 12964
Albuquerque, New Mexico 87195
www. EddieB.net
(505) 463-5080

Preface

A Focused Faith

We, as Christians, must make Jesus Christ the focal point of everything we do.

As believers, it is important that we glorify His name in everything we are part of.

Our Father redeemed us by sending His only Son, Jesus, to pour out His blood on the cross, to cleanse us from all sin, and to literally "buy us back," saving us from the end we so much deserved.

We have all heard of the great price that was paid for our salvation, but do we ever think about what being redeemed really means?

It means to pay the debt for, to release from slavery or captivity, to be freed from the consequences of, to save from harm or detriment, to pay ransom for, to buy back or repurchase. Meriam-Webster.com

God is holy, and He could not bring us back to Himself while we were still in sin. He had to provide a way to cleanse us of all sin and make us clean again, so that He could bring us back to Himself.

He knew that all of the blood of man was corrupted with sin, so He had to provide a pure and holy sacrifice to cleanse us so that we could be forgiven our sins and live with Him forever.

That is why He sent part of Himself, His only Son, Jesus, as our sacrifice.

From the moment that Jesus was nailed to that cross, shed His holy and sinless blood, suffered and died, and rose again on the third day, He has been the main *focus* for a changed, forgiven life.

If we will just accept His salvation from sin and death and ask Him to become the Lord of our lives, we can have a whole new life!

The moment that we are saved though, brothers and sisters, it is not *over*, it just *begins*.

We must remember that we are a "package deal," and God wants *all* of us, not just parts of us. He wants to be included in every part of our lives.

It is important for us to examine ourselves to see where the focus of our own life is directed.

I found when I examined myself, that I was focusing too much on watching that box we call a TV. As I began to focus more on the word of God, I noticed other things that had stealthily crept into my life as well, things that I knew, as a believer in Christ, I should be more careful of. This gave me a much clearer picture of where my walk was.

He said that the road is narrow that leads to life. When your sight "focuses in" on something, you narrow your view, so that you can *very clearly* see whatever you are looking at. It is just like when we use binoculars; our field of vision is narrowed to whatever we are trying to see distinctly.

If the "binoculars" of our *faith* are focused on Christ, we will bring everything concerning Him and our lives into a sharper view.

So, our minds should be *focused* on Him and His word. The care of our bodies should be *focused* on keeping His temple, our bodies, in good condition, our mouths (though the word clearly explains what a constant battle this is) must be disciplined to speak only those things that would bless others, edify, and bring glory to our King.

What then happens as we begin to focus our faith and the way we live our lives totally on Jesus?

As we focus all we are and have on Him, as we surrender to His will for our lives, we become more and more filled with the power of the love of Christ.

The Bible says the greatest of the gifts is love. Christ's love is unconditional; it perseveres, it does not quit, and it never changes. Although as fleshly beings our love is very fickle, the love of Christ within us is faithful and holy.

So then, what happens when we focus on His love and not our own? What happens when we begin to love other people with His love instead of our own?

We begin to change the world around us!

Wherever we are, whatever we do, we must be sure that we have Him in mind. When my kids were small, I used to tell them, "If Jesus can watch it or listen to it with you, if He can go there with you and take part in what you are doing, if you can say it in front of Him, or offer it to Him, then it's fine. But if you wouldn't want to invite Him along with you, or let Him see you taking part in it, then it's not all right, because when He lives in our hearts, we must remember that He goes everywhere with us."

One night we were playing cards with friends and I kept winning. One of our friends asked me what I was doing to keep winning. I said, "I'm cheating. I asked Jesus to play with me."

They said, "You can't ask Jesus to play cards with you!"

My answer was, "If I can't, then I'd better not be playing cards, right?" They had to agree.

When we have a focused faith, we also sometimes have to take a stand for that faith.

Many years ago, I was working as a receptionist and switchboard operator and a call came in for the owner of the business. I called his extension and he said to tell the caller that he was not in. I asked my boss if it would be all right if I told the caller he was not available instead. He agreed that would be fine.

Later my boss came by my desk and asked what had been the problem. He said that he was just curious.

I very respectfully explained that I was a Christian, and that I did not feel right about telling, what would be to me, a lie, because I knew he was in the office. He stared silently at me for a few seconds and then said that he was very glad I was working for him, because now he knew that I would also never lie to him either.

Brothers and sisters, people are dying every day all around the world, without the hope of spending eternity in heaven with our Heavenly Father. It is up to us to carry Christ's love to people who are in need, who are hurting, and who do not know how very much He loves them.

The hurting do not always search out someone to help them. First of all, they don't because they don't know who to go to. There are church signs everywhere, but if you are on the outside, you have no way of knowing that you will be welcome inside, especially if you are on the streets or an addict.

We have to go to the people who are hurting and reach out to them in the love of Christ. Remember that it is our arms, and our hands, that must represent His own as we reach out to souls that are so in need of His peace and His salvation.

Those who are incarcerated behind prison walls cannot reach out to us and ask us for help. We must go to them.

People also do not know who they can trust. When you are on the streets or incarcerated, you learn to trust no one, because that is what you must do to survive.

That is why it is so important for us to daily *walk* in Christ. Others will begin to trust us when they see the fruit of our own lives, as we live to glorify our Lord.

Jesus told us to go because He planned for us to go out and help those who are in need, just as He tells us in the Bible to feed the hungry, visit the sick, visit those in prison, and care for widows and orphans.

We must get out of the pews, brothers and sisters, and be about our Lord's business.

We must not let the souls of the very people Jesus died on the cross to save be lost forever! Even one lost soul is far too many!

Who will reach out to the hurting for Jesus? How about you?

If the issues in our world today such as the crime rate, the number of children who are abused today, the millions of children who daily have their lives ended before they even begin, the homeless, the hungry, all kinds of addictions that are taking people's lives—if these issues concern you, brothers and sisters, please remember that it is *God's people* who have been "commissioned" to go reach out and help in Christ's name.

If we want to help the crime rate, then we will need to go into the prisons and jails and take the love that changes lives to those forgotten souls inside.

If we want to help stop abuse, then we will need to reach out to families and single parents in need and offer our support, our help, and our mentorship.

If we want to help those who are suffering from addictions, we must reach out to addicts with the saving love of Christ and provide them with tangible support.

Brothers and sisters, *why* is it so important to live a life *focused* on Christ?

It is important because if we do, the power of Christ will set people free and will change the world around us!

The greatest power on earth lives inside our hearts! The love of Christ! But for it to make a real difference, we must give it away!

It is time, and past time, for us to let the power of Christ flow through us to the world.

We hold the key to change and freedom.

Arise, people of the living God and Christ, and take His love to the world!

I pray that this little book will bring you closer to Christ, will encourage you, and will inspire you to *a more focused faith* as you serve Christ.

In Jesus Christ our Lord,
Janet S. Williams

Introduction

IF ONLY ONE

If only one, Lord, if only one of your children,
By means of melody or word,
Would be caused to look up,
And see Your face.

If only one, Lord, if only one of Your sons and daughters,
Might hear in my meager rhyme,
A bit of an angel's song,
And go on to complete the race.

If only one heart could feel the peace in my own,
And reach out to grasp,
The treasures that await,
And be renewed.

If only one tempest-tossed, thirsty, trial-worn soul,
Could know the quenching powers,
Of Your rivers of living waters,
And call out Your name.

If only one lost child of the King could find his way home,
To the sanctuary of his Father,
And the waiting arms of his Savior,
Then the writing of the song,
Would not be in vain.

Praise Him

The Bible says that God inhabits the praises of His people.

When we begin to lift our hearts and voices to Him in praise, we can feel the change inside of us as He draws near.

It is easy to praise Him when everything is going well and we are happy, but it is much harder for us, it seems, to praise Him when everything is not going well and seems to be falling apart.

Yet, it is in these times when we need His comfort and presence the very most that we also need to praise Him.

Everyone knows the story of Paul and Silas and how they praised the Lord in shackles from their prison cells. What a great witness for us.

Many years ago, a beautiful Christian sister who was a close friend and her family, involved in an automobile accident. Her five-year-old son died soon after the accident, and when they came and told her that her precious little son had not survived, she lifted her hands and began to sing to the Lord.

The nurses thought she was having a mental breakdown in reaction to the news of her son's death and called the doctor. My beautiful sister in Christ explained to them all that her heart was broken, but that God was still God, and that she knew her son was now seeing the face of Jesus, the one he loved so very much, even at his tender age. She explained that her son was now safely home and that now the rest of the family must stay true to Jesus, so that someday they would be with him again.

What beautiful faith and love for God my sister in Christ displayed that day. Many people gave their lives to Christ because of her witness and the witness of her little son's love for Jesus.

Remember, brothers and sisters, you don't have to have a beautiful voice to lift in praise! The song that God hears in your heart as you praise Him is the most beautiful music on earth!

Oh Great and Powerful Lord, a Psalm

Oh great and powerful Lord,
King of kings and Lord of lords,
How wonderful is Your creation!
How magnificent is Your wisdom!

I regard with great awe,
The mysteries of Your handiwork,
From the flight of the Arctic tern,
To the bouncy kangaroo,
To the galaxies and mysteries of space,
Your glory is magnified!
All creation declares Your presence,
Your presence and Your plan,
I love You, Holy One!

Though Your power and glory,
Are far beyond my comprehension,
Your love more abundant than I could measure,
I praise You for allowing me to call You Father.

Your holy word is trustworthy and true,
Penned by Your own Spirit,
And I, creation of Your hand,
Taken from the dust of the ground,
And breathed into by Your own breath of life,
Rejoice!

I rejoice in the knowledge,
That You are God and Creator,
Alpha and Omega,
The First and the Last,
And through You,
I had my beginning.

I Worship You, a Song

In the early morning hours,
Just before the dawn breaks the sky,
I come and kneel before Your throne,
And worship You, God of Zion,
My heart unfolds before You,
And my soul lays bare before Your eyes,
In worship I lay at Your feet,
And Your Spirit renews me,
As the cleansing blood of Christ,
Washes me clean again,
Then because of this renewing time with You,
I go forth, and claim the day for Christ.

And If You Take Your Breath Away, a Poem

You are the Holy One of Israel,
Redeemer, Savior, and Lord,
You are the mighty God,
The Everlasting Father, the great I Am,
And if You should take Your breath away,
I would turn again to clay.

The sun, moon, and stars testify,
Of the power of the words of Your mouth,
And if You should take Your breath away,
I would turn again to clay.

In the crash and roar of the thunder,
I can hear the wheels of Your chariots of fire,
And in the splitting charges of electric lightning,
I see the power of Your messengers,
And if You should take Your breath away,
I would turn again to clay.

All creation testifies of the glory of its Creator,
Your magnificent beauty is beyond comprehension,
Your glory beyond definition or understanding,
Your power causes heaven and earth to tremble,
And if You should take Your breath away,
I would turn again to clay

You are the Rose of Sharon and the Lily of the Valley,
You are the bright and morning star,
You are the wind beneath the wings of eagles,
And *when* You take Your breath away,
I *will* turn again to clay.

Amazing Lord, a Song

You know what I need before I ask You,
You know how I feel before I say,
You prepare the way before each trial,
And hold my hand and keep me from day to day.

CHORUS

Amazing Lord, You hear my cries before they're uttered,
Amazing Lord, You'll always be my best friend,
Amazing Lord, You stand before me as a buffer,
Amazing Lord, what joy to know You understand.

You keep me through the dark with Your angels,
You guide me through the perils of each day,
When I'm attacked, You put Your hedge around me,
And gently guide me through the narrow way.

You're my Lord, my Savior, and my God,
You're my Father, the Rock, the great I Am,
But when my heart is weighed down, You are my Comforter,
Abba Father, the Everlasting One.

CHORUS

He Took Away All My Pain,
When I Began to Praise His Name, a Song
For Pastor Frank

Pastor Frank came to my house after he had pulled a piece of steel out of his hand due to an injury while drilling a well. He asked me to write a song using the words, "He took away all my pain when I began to praise His name," because the horrible pain due to his injury had left when he began praising God.

I was suffering in need of a touch from the Savior,
I needed healing from the Master's hand,
No other could hear my cries for deliverance,
No one else would understand.

CHORUS

I lifted my hands to heaven and began to worship and praise,
Then the peace of the Savior descended,
He took away all my pain,
When I began to praise His name.

Yes, the Lord delivered me from trial and suffering,
He lifted me in the palm of His hand,
He brought me out of the Land of Sorrow,
When my worship and praise began.

If you want relief from the cares of this world,
If you want to be healed and set free,
Lift your hands and worship, the God of Israel,
He inhabits the praises of His people.

CHORUS

God of the Impossible, a Song

Dear Father, sometimes the sky looks so cloudy,
And it seems that all it does is rain,
It seems that the sun will never shine again,
And my life, a hopeless trial of pain.

CHORUS

But I know, You are the God of the impossible,
And I know, You never leave Your children alone,
You are the One who makes my life livable,
My lifeguard on this angry sea so far from home.

So instead of crying, I'll sing Your praises,
I'll lift my hands in worship and praise,
For I know the God of heaven will never leave me,
And there's nothing You can't handle, Bless Your holy name.

Man of My Dreams

My husband and I came together because of the miraculous work of the Holy Spirit. I literally fell in love with my husband's name before I knew or fell in love with the man.

What drew me to my husband when we first met was his deep love for Christ.

My husband is my best friend, my encourager, my wise counselor, my joy, and the love of my life.

He has been through so many hard trials in this life, beginning with a very abusive home growing up and six years in prison as a very young man living through one of the biggest prison riots in history.

My husband is living proof, however, of how Christ can change lives. It has been twenty-three years since he was released from prison, and he has continued to follow Christ. He has never returned to his old way of life. He is one of the blessed ones.

My husband does, however, suffer from a chemical imbalance that causes depression and at times is very debilitating.

Our story is so much a part of my writing and our walk with God that I plan to share it in depth at a later time.

Let me just tell you this, though; some children of God do suffer from depression. But even when they do, they can still serve Him, walk with Him, and begin to heal through Him.

My husband has lived with depression since junior high, *but when he turned his life into the Savior's hands, the depression had to begin to obey the power of Christ.*

Last year I wrote and recorded a song about his life. I have included the lyrics here to give you a part of his story.

The Man of My Dreams, a Song
For my precious husband, Alphonsus

(He believed, he believed, he believed, that Jesus could set him free
He believed, he believed, he believed, that Jesus could set him free)

The little boy was crying, he'd been beaten once again,
So many times he had been struck down by his stepfather's hand,
And his mama couldn't help him, broken by beatings of her own,
And the little boy cried out to God to rescue him from his home.

The teenage son carried burdens far beyond his years,
He learned to make the streets his home and traded anger for his tears,
The harder he tried to get along and his new stepfather to please,
The more he was beaten down and brought to his knees.

The young man started taking things, things that were not his own,
Any way to make money to keep him away from his home,
And yet he hoped that someday God would take the fear,
That God would rescue him from hell, that God would surely hear.

(He believed, he believed, he believed, that Jesus would set him free)

The young man was crying, as he knelt there in his cell,
So young with five to twenty years, he'd traded home for another hell,
Yet even there his cry was heard, and Jesus held him tight,
And he broke all Satan's chains with salvation and love that night!

That young man who surrendered his life to Christ on that fateful night,
Sits here by my side, and I'm so proud to be his wife,
Jesus took the broken man caught in the devil's schemes,
And made him a new creation, turned him into the man of my dreams.

The very thing the devil had meant to destroy the soul of my man,
This cell of steel and bars, only brought him into Jesus' hand,
And that young man who once was lost and the devil had enticed,
Became a son of the Living God and led his mama to Christ!

(He believed, he believed, he believed, that Jesus had set him free)

And the man who surrendered his life to Christ on that fateful night,
Is right here by my side, and I'm so proud to be his wife,
Jesus took that broken man caught in the devil's schemes,
And made him a new creation, changed him into the man of my dreams.

(I believe, I believe, I believe, that Jesus saved him just for me.)

Daughters of the King

My precious sisters, we must always remember that our Father is the King of kings.

And it seems to me that if our Father is the King, that must make us, His daughters, like princesses.

I often think about the princesses I have heard about in stories and in life and about their characteristics.

It seems to me that most princesses are gracious, soft-spoken, respectful, well-mannered, deeply caring about others, and always mindful about their behavior, which most certainly will reflect on their Father the King and His Kingdom.

Princesses also seem to always be about their Father's business, and to be doing their best to take care of the people of the Kingdom.

Esther was a queen and we see all of these qualities in her. She was willing to lay down her very life for her people.

Sisters, we too need to be about our Father's business.

We need to help the helpless, bring hope to the hopeless, feed the hungry, clothe those who need clothing, and minister to the sick and brokenhearted.

I can tell you that my sisters-in-Christ have walked with me through some very difficult times. They have stood with me, encouraged me, took me in when I had no place to go, fed me, and kept me focused on Christ and His love. The bond between Christian sisters is one of the strongest in the world.

And if you have even one Christian sister who will stand with you through whatever may come, you have been blessed beyond measure.

May God bless you all, my sisters, and may the princesses of the Lord, our King, be a bright and shining light in His world, daughters of God and princesses of the King.

Daughters of the King, a Poem

We as Christian women need to remember who we are and how precious we are to our Father.

We are daughters of the most high God and sisters of Esther.

We are princesses of the King.

Have you felt like a princess lately?

Maybe you just need to take a trip into the throne room to see your Father, the King!

The King of kings and Lord of lords requests your presence,

Your presence every day to say good morning.

Every night to say good night,

Every loving daddy likes to kiss his little children goodnight and tuck them in,

Do you say goodnight to your daddy before you go to sleep?

Are you hurting?

Go and sit in a quiet place and let your Father hold you.

Are you happy?

Let your Father dance around the room with you!

Are you excited about your achievements?

Thank your Father for giving you the strength and courage to not quit!

Sisters, our Father longs to spend quality time with us,

To listen to the innermost thoughts and feelings of our hearts.

To comfort, encourage, cheer us on, and just hold us like when we were little.

Reach your arms up to Him today and let Him draw you close.

He loves you. He loves you! He *loves you!*

The King of all creation loves *you!*

Then we must remember what a princess does.

She stands for, and fights for, her people.

If you think of all the movies you have seen where princesses were involved,

Someone is always trying to get rid of the princess or control her.

Why?

Because a princess is the daughter of a king and will follow in the footsteps of her father to save her people.

Are *you* following in His footsteps to save His people?

Princess, a Poem

She wasn't much to look at, not as the world judges grace,
One hand didn't work just right, and there were scars upon her face.
Her hair had turned to silver, and her mouth showed the lines smiles had made,
She wasn't dressed in finery or fad, yet she walked with a regal gait.

And those who passed her on the street never stopped to say a word,
This little sparrow that the world thought lost had seldom a kind word heard,
Her head was bowed not in shame, but in reverence as she walked,
For this woman was the daughter of a King,
And it was of His kingdom that they often talked.

So many years ago, she had laid her life down, determined never to take it up again,
For the drugs and worldly lusts had beaten her down, and she felt there was no way she could get free of the sin,
Then one fateful night when she thought she was forever lost, she cried out, not wanting to be sentenced to hell,
And in a last desperation she cried out to God, and in that moment, into His everlasting arms she fell.

For when she let go of everything that the world had used to bind her flesh so tight,
And when she cried, "Jesus, save me!" she was washed with the blood of Christ that very night,
This woman who felt she had nothing left to give, and that all of her life had been lived in vain,
That very night became a new creature in Christ, and the daughter of the *king!*

And there are many women, young and old, whom you may not recognize for their stature in heavenly realms,
They look just like you, and just like me, but they are earthly representations of themselves,
For if you saw each one as they will be appear someday, dressed in a snowy white gown,
You would see the princesses of God the King, wearing their golden crowns.

Would you like to become a princess, one who, with the King, forever will reign?

Would you like to be washed as white as snow, become a new creation again?

Would you like to put on holiness and leave the emptiness and the fear behind?

Would you like to be the daughter of a King? Would you like to be set free tonight?

The King is calling His daughters to come out of the world, and to take their rightful place,

As holy women who will purify their lives, women who will be sanctified by His grace,

Are you tired of being a slave to the world? Are you done with the lies and the shame?

Then lay it all down and take Jesus' hand, and become a daughter of the *King!*

I Looked into the Eyes of Jesus, a Song

My life I'd lived on the streets, an outcast of society.
Scorned and despised, I walked in shame, but was unable to change,
For I'd never heard, "I love you" spoken from a true heart,
Until I heard it from Jesus, when He broke my chains apart.

CHORUS

I looked into the eyes of Jesus, and He did not look away,
He is the only reason I live free today,
He is the only one who looked on me with love,
He saw through the flesh of sin, into the heart within.

Like Mary Magdalene, I fell down at His feet,
But no gift I had to bring, no treasure for the King,
My Jesus smiled at me and said, "I love you just as you are,
The most precious gift I seek is the treasure of your heart."

CHORUS

I Didn't Know It Then, but I Know It Now, a Song

For my dad, the best father and most honorable and noble man I have ever known

She was only thirteen when her daddy died,
And she didn't comprehend forever then,
She just knew he'd never leave her, she knew he'd come back again,
She kept looking down the driveway for his truck to pull in.

CHORUS

The day her daddy died, Jesus took her by the hand,
He's walked with that little girl every day since then,
And when her tears fell like rain, He'd turn them to rainbows somehow,
She didn't know it then, but she knows it now.

Every little girl needs her daddy to hold her tight,
And to chase away the boogeyman in the dark of the night,
Who does a little girl run to when her daddy's not in sight,
Who will keep her safe until the morning's light?

CHORUS

Now that little girl's hair has turned to white,
She sits reading her Bible in the lamplight tonight,
She thinks about the nail-scarred hand that's always held hers tight,
And she knows that He'll be waiting when her soul takes flight.

LAST CHORUS

And the day my daddy died, Jesus took me by the hand,
He's walked with this little girl every day since then,
And when my soul leaves this earth, we'll walk home together through the clouds,
I didn't know it then, but I know it now.

God Save the Children

Dedicated to the boys and girls at YDDC.
We love you so very much!

So many children today are growing up without mamas and daddies to nurture and love them, or are being abused by the very parents who should be protecting them.

We as Christians can make such a huge difference in these children's lives by taking every opportunity to invite them to church, mentor them through established mentorship organizations, and being an example of Christ to their lives.

My husband and I usually carry Bibles in our car so that if we come into contact with someone who needs the truth of His word, we can give a Bible to that person.

I remember waiting in the car for my son one day as he went inside a store. I was playing Christian rap in our car, and I noticed that the young man sitting in the car next to ours was also playing rap music. It sounded like Christian music to me, and I asked him.

He said that it wasn't, but that he was a rapper and a long time ago had wanted to rap for the Lord. He had somehow lost his way but wanted to find his way back.

I asked him if he had a Bible, and he said that he had lost his when he had moved to our area. I went to the back of our car and got out a new Bible for him. He got out of the car when I offered it to him and was very surprised that I would just give it to him.

Big old tears rolled down his cheeks, and I hugged him. Then with his permission, I prayed for him to be strong and follow God's will for his life.

When my son returned and got into the car, I waved good-bye to my new friend, and he waved to me, giving me a big smile and a thank you.

I don't know what happened to that young man, but God does. I pray that a seed was planted that day that will grow with the Lord's guidance.

There are also so many of our children in detention centers or jail today.

These kids are hungry for a kind word and someone who cares enough to bring the word of God in to them.

We have volunteered with Conviction Ministries inside the walls for two years now, and it has been so rewarding. God loves these precious children so very much. It is such a joy to let them know that they have a Father who will never desert them, never walk away, never try to hurt them, who never changes, who is true and faithful and a Father who loves them so very much!

The thing that I have found inside the walls is that I come away so very blessed. When I was in the hospital this year, our kids inside were praying for me, even those who did not yet know me. God bless those precious kids who "prayed me through."

I urge you to reach out to our teens and children inside or outside the walls and give them the helping hand they need to live a holy life in Christ. They are the leaders of tomorrow, the mommies and daddies of tomorrow, and so many of them need a good example to follow. What better example than that of Jesus.

Is There a Shelter in Here? Who Can I Run To?
A Poem

I live in a jungle,
No, I don't live in Africa; I live in the United States of America,
But when you're a teenager, you know a person between the ages of thirteen and nineteen?
This life can be like living in the jungle,
And believe me, the wild animals here are sometimes fiercer than the ones in the real jungle,
Sometimes I just stay in my room and close everyone out,
I try to get deeper and deeper into my music,
Because when all I hear is the music, I can't think, or feel, or be afraid ...
When I start feeling the fear, I want to run,
Run away from all the animals that are coming to attack me,
All I see is sex and violence on TV,
Some of my friends have already been brought down by these animals,
They have babies or wonder if they have AIDS,
Or they're just dead, because somebody brought a gun to our school,
And didn't really comprehend *death!*
Drugs don't even have to be bought,
There's always somebody more than willing to give you a hit,
And when they say that it'll make you feel better,
I almost take it, but so far I haven't;
I'm trying to fight off the animals, but it's hard fighting them all by yourself,
And I don't know where to run where they can't find me, they're everywhere!
Is there no place to run?
I don't want to take drugs! I don't want to do bad things!
But if you don't become part of them, they'll just kill you anyway!
I can't even run home, because they're there when I get there,
The TV, the alcohol, the drugs,
My mom and dad have already been caught, and the worst animal of all,
no hope, has them in its jaws,
Is there no shelter for me? Is there nowhere to run? Who will save me?

I'll Find You, a Song

For all the little children who were not given the opportunity to live and become all that God created them to be ...

My precious little child,
I have watched you from afar,
Before you drew your first breath,
I knew every contour of your face,
Every smile, every frown,
I could hear the beating of your heart,
And I smiled at your baby sighs,
And looked into your eyes.

I guided your tiny feet,
As you took your first steps,
And laughed for joy,
When you spoke your first words,
I've been with you every hour, every day,
Every moment of your life,
You haven't always known I was there,
But I would never leave you,
I would never leave you,
It is only you, my child,
Who would try to run from Me.

But there is something you should know,
No matter how you try to escape My love,
My love will find you,
My love will find you,
And then I'll call your name,
And you will come to me,
And I'll hold you like I did,
Before you were born.

No matter what deeds you have done,
No matter how far you wander from home,
My love will find you,
My love will find you,
And bring you back to My arms.

The Children, a Song

Last night I had a dream about waves upon the sea,
Colored flashes of light flowing together,
And as I stood upon the shore, the waves came close to me,
And I saw the faces of the lost caught in the tide,
I saw our children lost and lonely inside, inside the walls.

T-shirts of brown, T-shirts of blue,
Colors the same, but each face a different hue,
They called out to me, and they cried for the truth,
And then God broke my heart open wide;
He broke it for His children inside, inside the walls.

On the streets of our cities, our children are being sacrificed,
For our idols of sin and greed we've made our children pay the price,
We've built monuments to self and pride, and our babies lose their lives,
And who will save the children, who will lead them back to Christ?

CHORUS

And the mommies and the daddies are crying, "Bring our children home,"
Grandmamas and papas are pleading, "Don't leave our babies all alone,"
And the children are lost and dying, lured away for the devil's gain,
How long will we stay silent, hide our faces from their pain?
How many children have to die, before we hear His voice again?

And the children are crying, "Who will save us from the devil's snare?"
Who will take them the truth of Christ, and show them that He's really there?
The walls and bars that hold them can't save their souls from captivity,
And released from a cell, can't save you from hell, only Christ can set you free!

He Said That He Loved Me, a Song

He said that He loved me, I thought, "What do you want?"
The world doesn't give love away; it always wants something back,
Everybody wants something, and I've nothing left to give,
Wrung out by life's trials, with no reason to live.

He said that He loved me, I thought, "How can I believe
That someone on this planet, would ever want me?
I've nothing to offer, just an empty shell,
A broken body and spirit, headed for hell."

He said that He loved me; I looked deep into His eyes,
I searched for the cunning, and all of the lies,
Was He like all the others that brought me down to despair?
But only compassion and forgiveness were there.

CHORUS

I fell into His arms like a wounded bird with no wings,
A tortured soul with no tomorrows, a hopeless, helpless thing,
He picked me up and carried me, and my soul began to heal,
He filled me up with His love, taught my heart how to feel.

Then Jesus took me, all of me that was left,
Held me close to His heart, hasn't let go of me yet,
He said that He loved me; it was the first truth I'd known,
His love my salvation, the only road home.

Jesus is holding His love out to you,
Won't you please let Him hold you, show you all that is true?
He takes broken vessels that the world throws away,
Makes a vessel that's holy out of the broken clay.

I believed that He loved me, and now He's talking to you.

My Love Will Get You Through, a Poem

I sat there in my lonely cell, cast away by the world,
And being so young and so afraid, I suddenly felt so very old and without hope;
Within that room where I could only look forward to spending all of my young life,
All of the pride and the fierceness that I had lived by for so long,
All of the smart talk and the "coolness" could not give me back one day of freedom;
There in that cell, I fell down on my knees and cried out at last … to God;
Suddenly there in my barren room, I felt I was not alone,
I raised my tear-stained face and saw … Him;
He was surrounded by light, bright, glorious light,
And its warmth penetrated to the very depths of my hurting soul,
As He stood beside me, I felt His love radiating from His heart to mine,
It was the greatest sense of love I had ever felt;
He laid His nail-scarred hand on my head as if I were a child,
And with soft eyes full of sadness, He began to speak;
"My child," He said, and His voice was like thunder and music all at the same time,
"I have heard the cries of your heart, and there are some things I've come to tell you,
These bars may keep you in, but they can never keep me out,
I will be here right beside you each and every day,
In the sunrise of each new dawning and the moonrise of each new night,
I'm here and I'll always be with you, every step, and every breath, all the way;
When you're lonely, call out my name and I will hear you,
When you are sad, I'll send the Comforter to you,
When you rejoice, I will rejoice with you, and even here … I'll give freedom to you;
For these bars may hold your body, but your soul is free in me,
And your soul is able to soar above these walls,
On the wings of cagles I will lift you up, and my Sprit shall be your strength, and my love will get you through it all."

27

See Me, a Poem

If I had one wish, it would be that you would see,
See reality; see what's here and now, see me ...
You see my colors, you see the red, you see the blue,
You see the way I wear my hair, the car I drive, the things I do sometimes,
But you never see what's real, you never see me ...
You never see the heart of the child that beats within the warrior's chest
You never hear its cries, it cries to be loved, to be accepted, and to be valued.
My heart needs to know that you are glad that I came to this earth,
Glad that I live, that I breathe, that I am...
I know I'm not perfect, I don't claim to be,
Although you sometimes claim you are ...
Sometimes the hunger overtakes me, the hunger to be touched in a kind way,
Just a touch from a hand that is not meaning to strike,
Although I'd rather have that than no touch at all ...
And the loneliness I feel is so real,
Even in the middle of a crowd, with all my friends around me,
I feel lonely, lonely for that reassurance,
That can only come from you,
But where are you? Do you hear my cries?
Though unuttered, they scream through the silence,
See me! See me! I'm here! See me!
Touch me! Love me! Give me hope!
But you are not there ...
So I have clung to my colors, to my friends,
The only things of substance I know,
Yes, and sometimes I just drop out,
Drop out on whatever will kill the pain,
Hoping that someday I'll wake up,
And you'll know I exist ...
Maybe, if I make a loud enough noise,
You'll finally hear, and open your eyes,
And see me, see me, remember me ...
I am your child ...

Christian, hear the cries of the children. Hear the cries of despair of the mamas and daddies. The harvest is plentiful, but the laborers are few.

Christian, where are you?

Living in Christ

We must live every day of our lives as examples of the great love and grace of our Lord.

It's not always easy, especially when the world does its best sometimes to make you want to completely "lose your cool."

Through His strength, comfort, and grace to us, however, we will be able to persevere.

He extends mercy to us so that we might extend it to others.

One sure way to get yourself on the edge of losing your cool is to allow yourself to run on empty. We cannot give away something that we don't have to give. So, we must daily draw on His love and spend time with Him, to be able to "fill ourselves up" with His presence.

If we set a little time aside (preferably in the morning, so that we will be ready for whatever we may run into that day) and pray, read the word, praise Him, and just listen (That's the time we stop asking Him and start letting Him answer. This is a little harder than the asking part.), then we will not be running on empty when that person on the interstate cuts in front of us or a colleague is rude or we've just been told the report we've never before heard about has to be in the boss's office within the hour.

Living in Christ is being prepared, being "prayed up," and knowing what the most important thing in this world is. That's living our lives daily as examples of Christ, so that others who do not know yet how much He loves them will want to know what makes us different from the chaos of the rest of the world. It is our living by His example that may allow us to love someone right into heaven.

And that, brothers and sisters, is the ultimate goal.

A Letter to Someone, a Poem

The local paper received a letter one day,
Dear Sirs:
(The handwritten note said)
Would you please print my letter in your paper? Lord willing someone will read it.

Dear Someone,
You took my car last night. I don't know why anyone would steal it, it sure wasn't much, and it had a bad clutch. But you see, that was the only transportation my kids and I had.
You see, I'm a single mom with three little kids, and I can't afford to buy another one. I haven't paid that one off yet.
Come to think of it, you took something more precious to me than my car last night. As I write this letter, I can see there is an empty spot on the coffee table, an empty spot that only my best friend in this world can fill. My best friend was right there on the seat beside you last night. I'll tell you what; you can keep the car, if you'll just bring my Bible back tonight.
You see, I've worn out its cover holding it through the years,
And its pages are wrinkled from all of my tears,
When everything seemed lost and I just couldn't cope,
I'd just open its pages, and I'd always find hope,
Jesus would reach out to me through His words all in red,
And His words of encouragement, always my hungry heart fed,
When we all missed our daddies, my little kids and me,
I'd read from the place where our Father told us how it would be,
When we all got home to His kingdom and we walked the streets of gold,
And never again would we feel all alone;
My life is written in the margins of that book,
The things that He showed me, every time I looked,
That book became my best friend and was a link to our heavenly home;
Won't you please bring it back; you can keep the car for your own.
Signed, I forgive you

Three nights later, her car sat in the drive,
The keys in the ignition, it had had a waxing besides,
And taped to the steering wheel, was a paper neatly wrote,
"Please forgive me, for this car I stole, and for me just leaving a note,
I've brought back your best friend, but I have to confess,
I read it all night, because I just couldn't rest,
Those words in red kept on calling out to me,
And I finally read them all, and now I'm different, you see,
I've brought back your best friend, but first I took some time,
To find one just like it, and make its pages mine,
Please forgive me for what I've done, and please try to understand,
The day I took your Bible and car, I became a forgiven man.
Signed, God bless you, from His new son. "

Walk On, a Song

I came to the cross and laid my burden down,
I found comfort in His love and peace that had no bounds
There He washed me clean, life and hope surrounded me,
I was content with John 3:16, for it had set me free,
Yet I heard Him telling me,
To walk on!

CHORUS

He told me (spoken)
Walk on! Walk on!
Walk on from the cross, but be sure to count the cost,
Take my love to the world, every man and woman, boy and girl,
Give them the word of life, and the Spirit's guiding light!
Tell them I'm coming for my own, and I will take them home,
And when they've come to the cross, and they know my blood has paid the cost,
Help them to walk on!

Stop ... Look ... Listen ... Stand, a Poem

Stop:
Stand in your place and allow the pounding of your heart to quiet.
He who holds the universe has His hand on His beloved.

Look:
What others cannot see or fathom,
In brilliant, crystalline clearness is known by the Father.

Listen:
The Spirit speaks in muted whispers,
To the innermost recesses of the hearts of His children.

Stand:
Though savage winds encompass, the eye of the storm is tranquil,
For the presence of the Almighty is found in the midst of every crisis.

Stop ... Look ... Listen ... Stand ... And Prevail.

The Whale Sandwich, a Song
I've learned a lot about living in Christ from Jonah

The Lord said go to Nineveh,
And speak to my people there,
But I drug my feet, and took a boat ride,
And a big fish, it went *Gulp!*

CHORUS

I won't ask questions anymore,
I'll just go where You say to go,
I won't make excuses, I won't lay low,
Being a whale sandwich is a bore!

There's nothing to do in the belly of a whale,
There's no windows to look outside,
There's no place to go and the air is stale,
So unto the Lord I cried!

CHORUS

Sitting in the heat beneath a tent,
Grumbling about my plight,
Watching the worm eat my shade,
Complaining with every bite,
Then I heard the swish of a mighty tail,
There midst the desert sand,
And I heard the sound of a mighty *gulp*,
And my attitude began to change!

CHORUS

Savior

"Savior, precious Savior, who laid down all of heaven to bring me home. Savior, precious Savior, you took my sin-stained life and made it white as snow."
—*Janet S. Williams*

The day that I gave my life to Christ, I was in the ladies Bible class.

I had been attending class with Sadie, a dear, sweet Christian woman in her sixties, who had been showing me films about the Bible and about Jesus every Saturday morning. I would take the kids with me, and she would have toys for them to play with while we talked about the films, and she always had cookies and snacks for them.

Even though I had attended church and Sunday school as a child, I began to really learn who God and Jesus were from that dear saint. She patiently told me of their love and explained the stories of the Old and New Testament to me.

I had been studying with her for a few weeks when we attended that Bible class one weekday morning.

The Lord began moving in my heart, and when the class was over, I asked the pastor who taught the class if I could give my life to Jesus and be baptized. The ladies were moving toward the door, and he called them all back. Sadie helped me to dress in the baptismal white robe and watched close by while the pastor led me down into the water and asked me if I believed that Jesus Christ was the Son of God.

I knew in my heart that Jesus surely was God's Son. That day, Jesus became my Savior and Lord.

I still remember the song we sang after my baptism. It is still very precious to me even now, after more than thirty-six years of walking with the Lord.

After thirty-six years, I still remember Sadie, the precious saint who cared enough about my soul to take time to teach me of His love. I often wonder, if she had not taken the time to teach me, if our children, who have all been baptized into Christ, would also have made their choice to follow Him.

Savior of All Men, a Song

The manger was silent, all the animals held their breath,
All creation waited for the blessed event,
Mary and Joseph prayed for guidance from above,
The Son of God soon to be born would show forth the Father's love.

CHORUS

Precious little Lamb,
Born in a manger in Bethlehem,
Holy Christ Child,
The Savior of all men.

Then suddenly through the stillness, a cry, an angel's song,
Told the creatures and all the earth, the Savior had been born,
Mary and Joseph, their faces all aglow,
Looked down into the face of Christ, God's only begotten Son.

CHORUS

The Human Heart, a Poem

Within the recesses of every human heart,
Lives an unquenchable need to be cherished and loved.

I, myself, have walked the winding halls of my own heart,
And heard the echoing of my own lonely footsteps,
While I searched behind closed and secured doors,
For a loving place to lay and rest;
Searched for warmth that would take away the chill,
For caring, that would ease the pain deep in my soul,
Pain so deep that only true, unbridled love could reach that far;
"Where?" I cried, "Where can I find,
A soul that will want to know mine and seek my heart's depth,
A soul capable of loving unconditionally,
A soul that will not judge my worth by my trials,
Or the lines weather-worn upon my brow,
Or the tears that stain my garments with holes;
Oh where is one living soul who will not cast me to the ground,
Or call me worthless, not worthy to be loved,
Or even to be cherished,
One who would even bemoan the vapor of my passing?
Is there no one to remember my name upon their lips?
Remember it with more than a callous utterance?"
Not one voice in the entire world replied as I walked the cold and dreary
winter street.
Not one voice in all earth came to my ears to speak for me ... no, not
one ...
Yet, I heard a voice,
A voice sweeter than honey on my tongue,
A voice softer than a slip of finest velvet,
That rested against my weathered cheek;
And this voice that spoke from heaven and not from earth,
Spoke of love, love for me, and called me by a name I had never heard,
Yet I understood that it was mine, and mine alone.

And the warmth of a love more powerful than heaven or earth,
Filled my empty heart from corner to corner and unlocked every door,
Leaving my heart open to receive and to be cherished,
And there, alone on the empty, wintry street of despair,
I found the one who wanted to know my soul,
To know me, and to love me,
Unconditionally for all of heaven's eternity.

There, Jesus heard my need and filled it with Himself,
And there I, a lonely scrap of humanity, a castaway,
A life torn and tattered from the harshness of the world's society,
Was welcomed into Christ's arms as a child of the King.

Reach Out for the Cross, a Song

Are you feeling weary, like you can barely make the day?
Your spirit feels so heavy; your body feels like it's wasting away,
You call out to Jesus to help you continue the fight,
As the world seems to crush you with the weight of its plight.

CHORUS

Reach out for the cross; hold onto its saving power,
Return to your first love; let Him fill you again with His love,
Feel the anguish and the burden slowly fade away,
As you lay all the world aside, and your first love reclaim,
Reach out for the cross, and return to your first love.

Are you busy for the kingdom, but spend little time with your King,
Are you feeling empty hearted, even though your labors aren't in vain?
Can you barely lift your hands to worship, praise, and sing?
It's time to turn around, my friend, and return to your first love.

CHORUS

Return to your first love, return to the cross,
Where your sin was washed away, where Jesus paid the cost,
Fall into the arms that held you when you were hopeless and lost,
Reach out for His saving grace, reach out for the cross.

CHORUS

Jesus Only Rap

I know you know just where I've been,
You can see the scars left on my life by sin,
And there was a time when I could not see,
The reason why God would want to save me.

I'd walked the road where demons led,
Into a world where I was left for dead,
Then a hand reached down and I grabbed it tight,
And Jesus, Jesus brought me back to life!

CHORUS

No, I'm not falling for the same old lies,
That wrecked my life, left my spirit dry,
I'm following the truth and all that's holy,
I'm following Jesus, Jesus only!

I've been in the pit and smelled of smoke,
But the power of the blood, all the chains of sin broke,
The sacrifice of the One who took my place,
Saved my soul, covered me with His grace.

CHORUS

Spoken:
It's hard to understand why He took my place,
The holy Son of God for a sinner like me, just another hopeless case,
But His love was greater than all my brokenness and pain,
He laid down His life to wash away every stain,
I've been bought back from hell by the One pure and holy,
So I'll follow Jesus, Jesus only!

CHORUS

I Saw the Lamb, a Song

Scarred and stained from the past, with nowhere to run,
No release from the pain that tore me apart,
Though no fault of my own, I carried guilt from a child,
Of things done in secret that left wounds on my heart.

CHORUS

Then I saw the Lamb, I saw the Lamb,
With hair white as snow, and scars on His hands,
He opened His arms, and I ran inside,
I saw my freedom, I saw the Lamb.

Oh what sweet release, to lay on His breast,
And let go of the burdens that were so hard to bear,
He took me back to a child and erased all the pain,
He dressed me in white, He washed away every stain.

CHORUS

Oh come to the Lamb, He's waiting for you,
He will wash you clean, before the day dawns anew,
Come and rest in His arms, where no fears from the past,
Can touch you again, be set free at last.

CHORUS

I've Finally Learned How to Fly, a Song

I grew up as a shadow child, never fitting in with the popular crowd,
At a distance I watched other kids play, didn't think they'd want me anyway,
When I changed from a girl to a grown-up gal, no one noticed how I had turned out,
And I guess that I thought it was supposed to be, that no one would ever notice me.

CHORUS

And now I'm here, in this place, where I've taken time to know His grace,
And I finally see all I can be, it's written in His love for me,
He's given me wings to take to the sky, to lift them wide and learn to fly,
I soar and glide lifted by His love; He lifts me up, to realms above,
And I've finally learned how to fly!

I was the quiet one in the back of the class, had the answer first, raised my hand last,
Never dared to dream that there would come a day that I would no longer be that way,
Now in this place I've reached out for the stars, and He's begun to heal my scars,
And the person I started out to be, well, that just wasn't who He intended me to be.

CHORUS

Have you ever been in that lonely place, where you thought you could never claim His grace?
And you thought God didn't know your name, that He and the world they felt the same,
Well I'm here to say He's not like the world, and He loves us lonely little girls,
And if you'll give your Father's love a try, He'll surely teach you how to fly.

SECOND CHORUS

And now you're here, in this place, so take some time to know His grace,
And finally see all you can be, it's all written there in His love, you'll see,
He'll give you wings to take to the sky, so lift them wide and learn to fly,
You'll soar and glide lifted by His love; He'll lift you up, to realms above,
And you'll finally learn how to fly!

REGULAR CHORUS

For Even One Like Me, a Song

He forgave me, before I knew Him,
On that cross so long ago,
He washed me clean with His own blood,
But I chose to say, "I never knew."

CHORUS

He came to save the human race,
And set all the captives, set the captives free,
He gave His life for all mankind,
For even one, one like me.

I denied His royal birth,
I mocked His glorious, His glorious throne,
From deep within the pit of hell,
I would not call out, call put His name.

'Through His love, He kept drawing me,
To His arms and to His peace,
Tired and weary of fighting, my Lord,
I surrendered to His, to His will.

Clean Again, a Song

There is nothing I can do about yesterday,
I cannot erase the things that I've done,
There is nothing I can do about my mistakes,
And all my guilt will not wipe away even one.

CHORUS

But the precious, cleansing blood of Jesus,
Flows over me and takes every sin,
In the crimson flood that poured on Mount Calvary,
I have been made clean again.

There is nothing I can do to pay the balance,
There is no way I can make up for the loss,
Of the many years I spent in rebellion,
To the Savior's saving grace upon the cross.

If there were one thing I would tell you, my brother,
I would tell you to lay it all before Christ,
Lay down the sin, the guilt, and the heartbreak,
For Jesus willingly, in love for us, paid the price.

Trust in Him at All Times, a Song

I was an orphan, a child with no mother,
A child with no father to call my own,
I felt unwanted, rejected, and worthless,
Downtrodden and hopeless, and so alone,

Then You saved me and called my Your daughter,
You were the Father I'd searched so to find,
Abba Father, you gave me faith and hope,
Your love is a treasure I so long denied.

CHORUS (Ps. 62:8)

Trust in Him at all times,
Ye people pour out your heart,
Before Him,
God is a refuge for us.

The pain and the heartbreak that you still carry,
My brothers and sisters, you've no need to bear,
Jesus is waiting to lift from your shoulders,
Each nightmare of torment, each burden of care,

Lonely people, there's comfort in Jesus' love,
He'll wipe away every tear, and bind up your heart,
The Son that the Father sent down here to save you,
Will never forsake you, will never depart.

A Diamond in the Makin', a Song

CHORUS

When you look at me, you will see a piece of coal,
But when you see me shining forth, from heaven's golden shore,
You'll know I've been through the fire, but I wasn't forsaken,
I was purified, sanctified, a diamond in the makin'.

Oh brother, please be gentle with this little child,
I know I often make mistakes and drive the family wild,
But the Master is workin' to refine this bit of clay,
When the Master is finished, I know I'll shine as bright as day,
I'm just a diamond in the makin'.

Oh sister, pray for me while I'm turning on the wheel,
That His hands will be gentle as my scars He starts to heal,
And when the pressure increases, and the gem begins to form,
Pray He'll rescue His creation and preserve it for its home,
It was a diamond in the makin'.

CHORUS

House of Sparrows, a Song

There is a house, a house of sparrows, built by the living God,
And in this house, this house for sparrows, sanctuary can be found,
Well in this house that welcomes sparrows is a place for the lonely and lost,
Where troubled souls and wounded spirits can find comfort for hearts weary and tossed.

CHORUS

Come to this house that welcomes sparrows,
We were counted as nothing by the world,
Deep in God's heart, there's room for sparrows,
And His Son has shown us what we're worth.

Let's storm the streets searching for lost souls,
Open every prison cell,
Gather all the treasure into God's house,
Every little sparrow tell.

CHORUS

Only Jesus, a Song

In many ways though I'm past a tender age,
I'm still a child deep inside,
And I need to be held and loved,
For the rivers are full of tears I've cried.

CHORUS

Only Jesus can put the pieces back together,
Only He can heal a ravaged soul,
Though I tried and tried to save myself,
Only Jesus could make me whole.

Those I loved only tried to destroy me,
Those I trusted tried to tear me apart,
When they failed, I tried to finish it myself,
For I believed their lies in my heart.

Many things have scarred my soul,
Many things have beaten me down,
But I've been put back together and made whole,
By the precious, loving friend I've found.

Stop Right There, a Song

My friend, I see you've been running for a long time,
Trying to escape the love of God,
Someday you will see that the very one you feared most,
Is the one you'll run to when the journey's done.

CHORUS

Stop right there! There's no need to run farther,
Stop right there! There's no place to hide,
The Father of Lights is all that you search for,
He'll give you rest and cast your fears aside.

Sometimes we fear that God is our enemy,
Sometimes we're afraid to surrender to His will,
But you will see that only in His love,
Will you find peace, will you ever feel fulfilled.

SECOND CHORUS

Stop right there! Your race has come to an ending,
Stop right there! You've been running uphill,
Come take the hand of the Father of Mercies,
Victory is sweet when you've done the Father's will.

It's Just Not Worth It, a Poem

We are faced with so many little tests in life,
Decisions, decisions on what to do,
And it really is all up to us,
We can, or we don't have to,
Whatever the test,
But we must live with the choices we make,
And it is these little choices,
That prepare us for the really big ones,
That will face us down the line;
So, before you take that drink,
Before you "light up" or "shoot up" for just one more time,
Before you indulge in that "little lie,"
Remember …
The choice you make today,
May affect the biggest choice of all someday,
Whether to spend forever in heaven with God,
Or eternity without Him,
Better start building up your strength now!
It's just not worth,
Not being able to go "all the way" on the Big One.

The Power of Christ

In January 2010, I laid in a hospital bed with a blood clot extending the entire length of my right leg. My right knee had been x-rayed and it was found that there was no cartilage, which was causing intense pain. I had just gotten over H1N1 and had acute renal failure, was anemic, and could not even get out of bed by myself.

I was horrified to look in the mirror because I looked haggard and on the verge of death.

I have always been the strong one, the one in control, the one who gets things done, and I had run for years on little sleep, not taking care of my body, and continually stretching the envelope of my health.

I had forgotten a very important fact. My body is the temple of the Living God, and I am to take care of it.

As I lay there, with all control ripped from my hands, I realized what I had done. Then I realized that my very life did and always had been in the complete control of God Himself. He had kept me all those years, even though I had been so foolish.

I realized that I had to give everything back to Him and let Him be God and do the very best I could to honor and obey Him. He deserved to be in complete control, not me!

God ministered to me in so many ways in that hospital room, through the staff, through other patients, through my family and my friends.

One night I was in such anxiety because they were going to go in and remove as much of the clot as they could the next day. I just couldn't calm down. Then one of the nurses came in to check on me, and I somehow began telling her how God had kept me all my life. As I talked, I remembered all of the times God had saved me from trials, from bad situations, from despair, and even had saved my life at birth.

As I found myself remembering His faithfulness, my faith began to recover and the anxiety left. The more I praised God's keeping power, the calmer I became.

Another night, my call button flew with a loud thud off my bed, even though I had secured it well, and when I came fully awake, I realized I was in trouble from my asthma and called the nurse. I know that one of God's angels surely awakened me.

Now at this writing, I am off Coumadin, I have put away my walker, I have put away my cane, I am exercising about twenty to twenty-eight miles a week, and I have lost thirty-two pounds. My doctor says that I look like a totally different woman.

I know that the power of the Living God saved me again and gave me my life back, and I am doing my very best to honor Him with my body and take care of it.

All I have, all I am, all I ever will be belongs to my Savior and my Lord, and I am only here because He saved me! My life is a miracle of the power of God and Christ!

I pray that I may bring glory to His name!

May all glory and honor and power be unto our God and to His Christ, His only Son, Jesus!

Sin Breaker, a Song

The devil thought it was over; Jesus had been nailed to the cross,
He'd seen the blood flow and watched Him die,
But as the devil laughed, he didn't realize,
That forever would be changed in the blink of an eye.

Jesus opened His eyes, sealed salvation for all time,
In that moment He sealed the devil's fate,
And we, who'd been stolen in that garden long ago,
Were redeemed and set free by His grace!

CHORUS

He's the sin breaker, the earth shaker,
He died on the cross and rose again!
The power of His blood can wipe away your past,
His name rips away the chains of sin!

He's the heart mender, the help sender,
Angels fly to your aid at His command!
He's the perfect sacrifice who paid your salvation's price,
He holds your freedom in His nail-scarred hands!

You can't fight Satan standing on your own,
You need Jesus to step into the fray,
He'll take back what you've lost, and all your sin has cost,
And all you have to do is shout His name!

CHORUS

If you want to be free from your chains today,
Just open your heart and say with me,
I'm tired of the sin, and all my life has been,
Jesus, Set Me Free!

CHORUS

You Have to Come through Me, a Song

Spoken:
In the beginning was the Word and the Word was God, and the Word was with God and the Word became flesh and dwelt among men.

Sung:
I am the shepherd, who watches over the sheep,
The ones who washed their robes and were sealed,
I laid My body down across the entrance to the fold,
Where they've been made whole and been healed!

CHORUS

They've been washed in the blood, sealed by the Holy Spirit
Their names have been written down in glory!
They are prophets and priests, warriors and conquerors!
And if you want to take My lambs, you have to come through Me!

Spoken:
I am the good shepherd: the good shepherd gives His life for the sheep. I am the good shepherd and know my sheep, and am known of Mine.

Sung:
I heard you've been hunting them like a lion in the night,
Seeking whom you can devour,
But those who have been washed in my blood are Mine,
And you'll never take them out of My hand!

CHORUS

My sheep know My voice, and hearken to My word,
They know that My love has set them free!
I will come to rescue them, when they call My name,
And one day I will bring them home to me!

CHORUS

Spoken:

I am the Alpha and Omega, the first and the last, and one day everyone will bow their knee,

I am the Lamb who was slain, and who rose again, and at My name demons must flee!

And if you want to take My lambs, you have to come through Me!

Access Denied Rap

Everywhere there are passwords that you need to get inside,
Everything that's important has a code you must provide,
And if you don't have the password, then entrance is denied,
And only Jesus has the password to get into my life!

CHORUS

My mind is sealed,
My heart is sealed,
My soul is sealed,
My body is sealed,
So Satan, if you try to bring sin into my life, and if you come to tempt me
with your lies,
Only Jesus paid the price to come inside, and Satan as for you, ***access denied!***

When I gave my life to Jesus, He sealed me for all time,
He took the Lamb's book of life, wrote my name on the line,
Now I'm surrounded by His angels, and the word renews my mind,
And I'm "password protected" until the end of time.

CHORUS

Spoken:
Ephesians 1:13: In whom ye also trusted, after that ye heard the word of
truth, the gospel of your salvation: in whom also after that ye believed, ye
were sealed with that Holy Spirit of promise.

CHORUS

Soldiers of Christ

Recently, my husband and I were passing a convoy of American soldiers on the interstate highway. We saw young men in camouflage gear, their helmets strapped on, and their eyes intent on the vehicle in front of them.

Occasionally as we passed, we could see their animated conversation, or hear a young voice laugh.

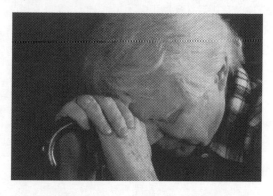

I smiled, thinking of our own sons and the sound of their laughter.

Then a great heaviness came over me, a great sadness, and I began to weep, but I did not know why. My husband looked at me questioningly, and I said, "I'm sorry; I have this sudden urge to cry." Then I said, "I feel like some of these young men will die."

The heaviness was overpowering like a great weight, and then I thought I heard the Lord speak to me, "These are like my soldiers."

I thought that the Lord meant that Christians were dying in battle, the battles being waged around the world for the cause of Christ and the preaching of the gospel.

But then in my mind, I saw soldiers in full battle gear, standing straight and tall, steadfastly looking ahead to what was surely to come. They appeared to be waiting for the onslaught of a battle. Their eyes did not waver. They stood silent yet expectant, their feet firmly planted; shoulder to shoulder, they waited.

Then I saw the enemy as they rushed toward the soldiers. The army was large, dark, and menacing. The faces of these soldiers grotesque and evil, and I thought that they appeared to be an army of demons. They came in a thundering horde, rushing toward the soldiers who stood waiting.

The soldiers did not flinch or move from their places but stood watching them come, their faces set toward the enemy, their expressions resolute and sure.

I noticed that the enemy army was armed with many weapons, but that the soldiers, who stood waiting side by side, carried none. Their arms hung empty at their sides as they waited. I was astonished and horrified.

Suddenly, as the enemy was surely to overtake the brave soldiers where they stood in their places, I saw one of the soldiers kneel, bow his head, and close his eyes. He then extended his arms toward the enemy bearing down on him and his comrades. In his hands, he held out in front of him the word of the living God, the Holy Bible.

The soldier did not speak; he did not move. He did nothing but kneel there as if in prayer and hold out the word.

I was astonished at what I saw, and I felt my heart bursting inside of me, with the love, the faith, and the peace I felt radiating from this soldier as he laid down all that he had in humbleness for the Lord.

At the same time, I looked back with weeping to see what the evil army would do as they faced the purity of this soldier's faith and obedience even in the face of possible death.

In great surprise, I saw that the land that lay before the soldier now had become completely empty. Not a trace of the evil army remained. Peace lay across the land and embraced it. As the soldier of Christ had held out the word of God toward the enemy, they had vanished!

The soldier slowly stood and looked at his companions. No one spoke, but all raised their eyes to the sky above them. As they looked up toward heaven, I could see shining on their faces the deep love and worship that filled them all. The love was so all-encompassing that it had enabled them to lay everything down at the feet of their King and to trust completely in the power of their only weapons, the word of God and prayer, to give them the battle.

Beloved, I believe that God wants His children to remember how to stand as soldiers of Christ the King and to win the battles that we are faced with living in today's world.

Beloved, remember that soldiers of the King know the power of the holy word of God and the power of the words, "It is written."

They know the manifestation of His word, the Living Christ, Jesus, the Lamb of God, and in Him they live and move and have their being.

They know the power of the Holy Spirit and welcome His presence, guidance, wisdom, and anointing. They know the cleansing power of the blood of Christ and the cross.

They know that the spoken word of God does not return void and that the truth of the gospel of Christ has the power to heal those whose ears cannot hear and open the eyes of those who cannot see to salvation.

They know the battle is not their own but the Lord's.

They know that keeping your life according to your own will is to lose it and that surrendering your life and will to the will of God is to save it.

They know that true surrender is to allow the word and the love of Christ to overcome your enemies.

They know that a soldier without knowledge of the truth and the word of God will not be able to stand and defeat the enemies he or she will surely face.

Soldiers of Christ, the word lives and moves among us. He sanctifies, purifies, heals and restores, strengthens and sets free the imprisoned heart and soul. His love and His shed blood on the cross save those that were lost without hope. He gives an eternal inheritance to all those who will accept His gift of salvation and life.

You who are His are known by His love being manifested in your lives! The word of God and prayer are your constant companions.

The Lord knows that you stand at the ready to minister healing to the broken, to give hope to the hopeless, to free those in bondage, to let those who have been locked away know that they are not forgotten, to feed and clothe the widows and orphans, to hold the sick and dying, and to do battle for the souls of the lost. He knows that you lay down your own lives for the sake of others.

One of the greatest warriors of Christ that I know is a ninety-three-year-old sister in Christ who daily prays for everyone she knows and all of her neighbors. Her life is a lighthouse of faith to everyone around her.

Soldier of Christ, beloved of the Father, you are not alone. The Lord Jesus is always with you, and I your brother, and I your sister, stand beside you. Remain ready for battle dressed in the whole armor of God and know that together we will stand. Stand and see the deliverance of the Lord, our King.

Warriors of Christ Rap

The enemies of God are waging war,
God said in the last days it'd be as before,
Violence and hatred would again rule the land,
And the perishing would cry for a Savior's hand.

The demons of hell using sin and drugs for chains,
Consume the hearts of men covered with stains,
Then as hope seems lost for those who cry in the night,
The army of the Lord steps into the fight.

CHORUS

As the warriors of Christ go to their knees,
*They speak out the **word** and the enemy flees,*
The demons of hell run away in shame,
As the army of God cries Jesus' name!
Jesus! Jesus!
Every knee must bow, at the sound of His name,
The First and the Last, the Savior, King!

As the demons of the enemy in a thundering horde,
Rush in flames toward the army of the Almighty Lord,
The warriors of the King kneel; the Holy Spirit is heard,
And the enemy is vaporized by the Living Word.

CHORUS

A Different Kind of Soldier, a Song

No, you cannot see his armor; he has no uniform of green,
And the fiercest battles sometimes are fought while praying on his knees,
The only weapon he carries is the holy word of God,
A sword that sears the hearts of men with fire from above.

CHORUS

He's a different kind of soldier; he fights his battles on his knees,
The armor that he wears you cannot see,
He has no uniform or medals bright; he's covered with the blood of Christ,
And when the war is over, he'll receive a crown of life,
He's a different kind of soldier.

This soldier that I'm speaking of is a strange one indeed,
If you smite him on one side, he'll turn the other cheek,
If you hurt his feelings or break his heart, he'll only forgive,
He's a soldier that carries the mark of Christ and helps others to live.

Soldiers of Victory, a Song
For Sandy. I miss you, Sis.

The battle is raging, opposing forces face to face,
There are soldiers dying, but another fills the space,
The white banner of Jesus flies high above the throng,
Hang on, my brothers, our Commander won't be long.

CHORUS

Soldiers of victory, sons of the living word,
The battle belongs to Jesus; He's coming for us on high,
Keep on; keep on, my brothers,
Listen for the victory cry.

Sometimes I am wounded, and I feel like giving up,
Like a roaring lion, the devil seeks to devour me,
But wait, the lion of Judah, the holy Lamb of God,
He's already won the war; to victory He holds the keys.

CHORUS

Shoulder to shoulder, and heart to heart we stand,
We are overcomers, winning hand in hand,
Keep on, keep on, my brothers, keep fighting 'til the end,
Jesus is holding each soldier in His hand.

CHORUS

Talking with My Father

I am still holding my daddy's hand even after all these years …

Oh, how I love you, Daddy.

Your little girl, Janet

It was so much easier for me to fall in love with my Heavenly Father, because my earthly father was such a wonderful example of a father's love, compassion, and character.

My dad stood only about five-feet-four, but to this little girl, he was a giant of a man. He was an immigrant from Czechoslovakia, and he loved America with all his heart. Dad believed in honesty, in always being fair, doing your very best with what you had, helping others who were in need, standing up for the underdog, and taking a stand for what was right and good.

One of his favorite sayings was, "Just hold out a little while longer." He was a man who knew how to persevere. Dad also felt that you should never judge a man until you had walked in the shoes that he had.

My dad was the kind of man who would come in the door after work, grab me up in his arms, and waltz around the living room with me. He always had a smile, he loved to whistle, and everyone was his friend.

When I was a child in the 1950s, dad found out that one of the cafes in our little town would not serve a group of people because of the color of their skin. Dad proclaimed that we would never again enter that establishment, because we would not support anyone who would refuse to feed someone who was hungry because of the color of their skin. He felt that the Good Book said that we were all equal.

Honestly, I am really here now because of my dad (both my earthly father and my Heavenly Father). When I was being born, the doctor said that he could not save both my mom and me and that one of us would not survive.

Dad told him that he had to save both of us and there just wasn't a question about that. We both made it!

I always felt that from the day I was born Dad took one of my hands and placed it in God's hand. That way, my dad held one of my hands, and God always held the other. Then when I was thirteen, and dad had to go on to heaven, he gently let go, but left his little girl still holding her Daddy's hand.

A Prayer

Dear Father,
You have shown me,
That You want changes in my life;
Being weak of flesh,
I am afraid, Lord,
But being filled with Your Spirit,
I am eager to run after You;
I deliver into Your hands,
My life, my all,
To do with as You will,
For You are faithful,
And trustworthy,
Your love is perfect,
Your mercy endless,
I will give to You,
My Master, my Teacher,
My beloved Father,
All my praise, all my love,
And I will do my best to serve You,
All the days of my life,
And especially now, into the unknown,
I will bravely walk,
Toward the sound of your voice,
My ear listening only to Your Spirit,
My heart responding:
"I am a willing captive, My Lord"
May Your will be done in my life.

You Are My Everything, a Poem

Some people speak of you in great "oratorical" tones,
And they are so "eloquent" in their prayers,
But I am not able to speak that way,
So my prayers are simple ones,
They often are more like a conversation than a prayer,
Just me, talking to You, and knowing with my heart,
That You hear me;
I know that even though You sit upon a glorious throne,
You hear my feeble cries; You feel the quivering of my heart,
And You taste my tears;
You, the King of the universe, take time for me, a small voice,
Crying out to the Father;
And some speak of You in great hushed tones,
Reverencing the very sound of Your name,
I bow before You, knowing you are Sovereign Lord,
I worship You and adore You, acknowledging who You are,
But ... You are so much more to me;
There are times when You pick me up,
And You just hold me, and comfort me,
And there are times when songs about You,
Rock me to sleep, just as if I was held by You,
When I am frightened, I run to You, my Protector,
When I am sad, I run to You, my Comforter,
When I am unsure, I run to You, my Counselor,
And when I feel unloved, I run to You, my Father;
Those times, as Jesus did, I call You Abba, Daddy,
For You are my Parent, my Daddy,
The one every little child runs to in time of peril,
And though I am grown, with children of my own,
I know that to You, I am still Your little child,
Always falling down and scraping my knees,
And still You bind up my wounds and help me to stand again,
Even after all these years;
I know I come to You with so many things,
Sometimes people have told me that I "bother" You too much,
But to whom would I go if not to You?

There is no one else who knows me like you do,
No one else who loves me as You do,
No one else has the answers like You do,
No one else … is God …
So, to me, you are Father, Counselor, Teacher,
Comforter, Doctor … Everything …
You, Lord, are my everything, and I thank You,
For being everything, to me.

This Heart, a Poem

This heart has been tossed about,
Like a ship without a rudder, riding on angry seas,
This heart has traveled many paths of promise,
Only to find emptiness at the end,
This heart has been seared and scarred,
Yet within its recesses still beats the promise of hope,
Hope that before it fades and grows silent,
It should know the joy,
Of true love experienced, and returned,
This heart has dreamed wistful dreams,
Dreams that appeared would never become reality,
Until You, Lord, have fulfilled them all,
And this heart,
For the first time in all its existence,
Knows what it feels like,
To truly … be loved.

When I Needed You, You Came, a Poem

I know You've been with me right from the start,
I've heard Your voice within the depths of my heart,
Somehow You knew there'd come a time when only You,
Would be the One I'd need to cling to;
When I needed You, You came,
And held me close to You, when I called Your name,
You saved my life, and set me free,
And now I dedicate my life to Thee.

Doors, a Poem

I have been told, Lord,
That when one door closes, You open another,
But what about those times,
When you don't want the door to close,
When you fight with every last little bit of strength,
To keep it open, even just a little,
Just a crack, so we can see a ray of hope,
Somehow, sometime, someday,
Not wanting to let go of what's behind that door,
Not wanting to see what's waiting,
Behind the door You will open,
Not wanting to know the end, and the new beginning;
Well, it's at these times,
When our hearts are bruised and scraped,
From the struggle to keep the door open,
That You sometimes take control, Lord,
You pry our fingers loose,
And gently, but firmly, close the door;
We are then outside the past,
But have not yet arrived at our future,
And it is this place we fear the most,
A place where we must come,
Face to face with ourselves,
And … with You;
This place where growth
And healing and learning occur;
I know that when You open that new door,
I will be glad that I spent time with You,
And with myself there in that place,
It's just that right now,
Walking through that door to a new beginning,
Is very scary, and I'm frightened,
So please, Lord,
Keep a tight grip on my hand,
Because I know,
That I cannot do this without You.

My Precious Child, a Poem

You are going through stressful and difficult times,
Do not let the stress overcome you …
At times the world seems to press in on you from every side,
Do not let the pressure overcome you …
You fear for loved ones and things you cannot control,
Do not allow the fear to overcome you …

Remember at all times,
That my name is I Am,
Not I Was … Not I Will Be …
But I Am …
Today, you and I together will handle whatever comes our way,
Hand in hand, we will face every trial, every hardship,
We will walk down the path of life together,
And whatever happens …
I will be there with you,
I will hear every beat of your heart, and every whispered thought,
My heart has tasted every tear you have shed,
All things … all things … are in My hands,
Trust Me even now … and relax in My care,
Let My love … overcome … everything concerning you.

Taken for Granted, a Poem

Sometimes a person just needs a little time alone, I guess,
Although it isn't what you always want,
Or "think" you need,
And it's funny,
But suddenly, all the things,
You thought were really important,
Mean absolutely nothing,
And the things you always took for granted,
Mean the whole world,
Like You, Lord,
You are my world, my sky, my breath,
And I will never, ever, take You for granted again

Sanctuary, a Poem

You know, Lord, having been born into our world,
And living and dying among us,
That life on earth is not always fun or easy,
You have know the great joy life is capable of giving,
But also the deep sorrows that can rend your heart,
To be able to live here, far from my home in heaven with You,
I have created for myself a sanctuary,
It is a place where I can drink from the crisp stream of living water,
Water only You can supply,
The only water that is able to quench the thirst of my parched soul,
It is a place where I can rest my weary body,
Leaning into the curve of Your arms,
And allow the sweetness of the Holy Spirit,
To replenish, nourish, and heal my wounds and scars,
It is a peaceful valley of silence,
Where the only sounds are the whispered brush of wings,
As your angels come close to me and surround me with Your protection,
And the song of praise that begins to be born in my heart,
As You, my Father, surround me with Your holy peace and serenity,
My sanctuary is what protects me from the insanity of the world,
It revives, replenishes, and relieves my stretched and battered being;
There in sanctuary with You,
I find the courage to go on living and to keep on trying,
To keep getting up when I fall, and to overcome;
You, oh Lord, are my sanctuary,
And my hope when all hope is lost,
There, away from the world and all its demands,
I am able to just be me, the person you created me to be,
Not the person that the world expects me to be,
And I am free to breathe, to rest,
And to turn off the noise in my head,
Created from constantly trying to meet the needs of others,
And You, my Father, my Savior, fulfill all my needs,
For You are my salvation, You are my hope,
You are my strength; You are my strong shield and fortress,
You are my God, You are my sanctuary.

The Love of Christ

What can be compared to the love of Jesus Christ? Nothing. Absolutely nothing.

There aren't even words in any language on earth that can fully describe His love.

We can say it is magnificent, glorious, never-ending, abundant, all-encompassing, miraculous, but to be very honest, it is absolutely beyond what any human being can fathom.

The book of John says that the word was from the beginning and that it was God and was with God. That means that the word that became flesh and lived among us, Jesus, left all of heaven's glory behind for thirty-three years just to come and live with us, to live like us, to know us, and then to die for us.

He traded streets of gold to walk in dust; He traded being right there with the Father, the King of kings, to live and walk and talk with us— we who were full of sin.

He took our sins upon Himself that we could be made clean.

He even cried to the Father to forgive us when He was nailed to the cross and pleaded that we didn't know what we were doing! He took our place upon that cross! We deserved it; He didn't.

And yet, only He, the holy Lamb of God, could love us enough to choose to give His own life, to pay the great price for our souls.

"Oh how great and wonderful is Your love, Lord! You are worthy Lamb of God, to receive all honor and glory and praise! Every knee must someday bow to your holy name. And all of heaven Your majesty acclaims!"

A Whisper of Wings, a Poem

My Father knows my every need,
And feels my every care,
He tastes my teardrops with His heart,
And comforts every fear.

And as I journey here and there,
Upon life's many paths,
He sends His angels along my way,
To care, and keep me safe.

In times of trial, when tested sore,
And with heaviness, my heart sighs,
I hear the whisper of hovering wings,
As angels 'round me fly.

And often times I catch a glimpse,
Of a feathered wing in the sun,
Or feel the breeze upon my face,
As they pass by on their rounds.

Then when my time upon this earth,
Has reached my final day,
I'll rejoice in the whisper of angels' wings,
As they carry me away.

Life, a Poem

I have my ups, I have my downs,
Some days I'm flying high, with my head in the clouds,
Some days my chin scrapes the ground,
And on these low days, the days I feel like,
The bottom has dropped out of my world,
And I'm hanging from this planet,
By a tiny thread, ready to spin off into space,
I am the worst friend that I have,
Grilling myself over and over about things,
That I should have done or not done yesterday,
Or two years ago, or two months ago, or even two days ago …
And all I succeed in doing,
Is making myself feel guilty, and sad, and regretful,
About things I cannot go back and change, ever …
Then there are the high days, the days that I admit to myself,
That today is a brand new day, that the future is a new beginning,
And that there is a God, a God who guides my life,
A God who loves me just as I am,
With all my frailties and my faults,
A God who forgives me my mistakes and shortcomings,
And helps me grow and learn from them;
It's these days when I lay down my life,
In His hands, totally, unconditionally,
That I am able to walk in the Spirit,
To hold my head up, to see the sun, the blue sky,
To hear the song of birds and buzzing bees,
And smell the tender, sweet scent of spring blossoms,
It is on these days that I *live* life,
And not just *survive* it;
You know what?
It's time to look up more, and back less,
It's time to live more, and think less,
It's time to bask in the warmth of His love,
And let His tenderness fill me up,
It's time to go on,
As He would have done, as He did.

This Is the Day That the Lord Has Made, a Poem

This is the day that the Lord has made,
And this morning my thoughts drift far away,
To the day like this, when another's eyes,
Looked up into the crystal blue sky,
Pondering the passing clouds,
And another's ear delighted,
In the cheerful, trilling sound of a songbird;
The breeze that caresses my cheek,
Touched His also,
He could see it dancing through,
The newly sprouted leaves of the tree in its passing,
And perhaps He smiled,
He could have knelt as I,
To enjoy the sweet smell of a rose,
Or tilted His head,
To glimpse a scurrying, tiny creature hiding beneath a rock;
Just as I, He went about His daily tasks,
But perhaps, looking at the sky more often,
Suddenly detecting the brush of angels' wings;
Just to know He was here,
Walking upon this earth,
Laughing, talking, crying, praying,
Somehow makes this day extra special;
Just knowing He came,
Makes the sun brighter, the bird's song sweeter,
And life ... a precious joy;
This is the day that the Lord has made,
My precious Lord Jesus,
I rejoice in it ... because of You.

Trust in Him at All Times, a Song

I was an orphan, a child with no mother,
A child with no father to call my own,
I felt unwanted, rejected, and worthless,
Downtrodden and hopeless, and so alone,
Then you saved me and called me your daughter,
You were the Father I'd searched so to find,
Abba Father, you gave me faith and hope,
Your love is a treasure I so long denied.

CHORUS: (from Ps. 62:8)

Trust in Him at all times,
Ye people pour out your heart,
Before Him,
God is a refuge for us.

The pain and the heartbreak that you still carry,
My brothers and sisters, you've no need to bear,
Jesus is waiting to lift from your shoulders,
Each nightmare of torment, each burden of care.

Lonely people, there's comfort in Jesus' love,
He'll wipe away every tear, and bind up your heart,
The Son that the Father sent down here to save you,
Will never forsake you, will never depart.

The Master Conductor, a Poem

The Master Conductor raises His hands,
Signaling for each member of His mighty orchestra,
To give Him full attention;
The murmuring ceases,
Every eye turns in eager anticipation,
To the face of the Creator
Of the piece about to be performed;
As the Master begins the piece,
Each instrument comes to life,
Breathing the very essence of the powerful melody,
The bass, the flute, the clarinet, the piccolo,
Each instrument adds its own special tone,
To the tapestry of sound, of light, of joy;
Then, as the song builds to its crescendo,
Light fills the space around the players,
And the very day is birthed,
In praise to the Master Conductor,
It is then that He directs the song to continue,
But with a softer, lighter, more-lilting tempo,
And He whispers to His band of faithful musicians,
"Carry on, sing to My children";
Then He smiles, the Master,
The Creator of the sweetest melody on earth,
At each tiny, upturned face,
And His tiny musicians,
His array of bright-winged birds,
Fan their wings, and softly, sweetly … joyfully,
Waken God's children, and His earth, from sleep.

So Close to Me Lord, a Song

I can feel Your presence in the air tonight,
My spirit feels your breath and reaches out to take flight,
I can almost see Your face there among the stars,
I feel Your Spirit in the quickening of my heart.

CHORUS

You're so close to me, Lord, and I can hear your voice on the wind,
"Watch and pray, My child, because I'm coming back again.
And then I'll hold you, and you will be with me forever."

I look up into the heavens, and I know that You are there,
You're looking back at me with so much love that I can hardly bear,
To keep my feet tethered to the earth and remain until You come,
But I know I must stay here for You as long as there is one who needs
Your love.

CHORUS

I look up into the heavens, and I know that You are there,
You're looking back at me with so much love that I can hardly bear,
To keep my feet tethered to the earth, and remain until You come,
But I know I must stay here for You as long as there is one who needs
Your love.

CHORUS

Marriage

Many years ago when Pastor Frank conducted our wedding ceremony, he told us, "Jan, if you have a problem with Al, don't nag him about it. Take it to the one who can change him. Pray for him. And Al, if you have a problem with Jan, take it to the one who can change her. Pray for her."

I have always remembered those wise words and have tried to make them a very important part of our relationship. The one problem, however, is that every time I go to the Lord to pray about my husband, the Lord always ends up showing *me* how I need to change. The beauty of it all is that the more I change, the more we both change, and our relationship in turn just keeps growing and becoming more wonderful.

One thing that has been a help to our relationship from the very beginning is that if we disagree (and I mean disagree, we do not yell or fight with each other), we never, ever, call each other names. We decided from the very start that not only were we husband and wife, but as Christians, we were also brother and sister in the Lord. That means that if we would not say it to a brother or sister at church or our pastor, we can't say it to each other either. Respecting each other in this way has built strength in our relationship.

We both have a great sense of humor, and that has been a great blessing to our relationship. Sometimes when I have been "disagreeable," Al has done something totally silly that made me laugh. Humor, in the right way and at the right time, can be a great diffuser. It's just very important that you both think it's funny, and that you laugh together, never at one another.

Another thing that we decided was that God's word, the Bible, would have the last say in any disagreement. You know there really aren't very many things, if any at all, that the Bible doesn't cover. It most certainly covers how we are to act, live, treat each other, and respect our mates. Even finances, which are one of the biggest reasons that people have arguments, are covered in the word.

If one of us is going through some "stuff," we try to gently encourage each other with the word.

Real strength in a marriage is developed through the threefold cord of husband, wife, and Christ together.

Today, the divorce rate is rising to a phenomenal level. Before you quit, throw in the towel, and walk away from your marriage, invite Jesus into the relationship. You might find your marriage totally turning around as you both grow in Him.

I told my husband not to ever think about getting a divorce because he had drawn a life sentence, and we were in this for all eternity!

I'm not going to say that it's always perfect for either of us, but we have made the commitment for the long haul, so whatever happens, we're just going to have to work through it with Jesus' help!

Jesus Binds Us Together, a Song

Today our lives are bound together forever,
With golden thread held in the Savior's hands,
No more twain, but as one flesh we shall praise Him,
And walk the pathway to heaven hand in hand.

CHORUS

And Jesus shall be the One who binds us together,
In the light of His love we'll learn and grow,
Our lives are sealed from this day forth and forever,
For what God has joined shall remain, forevermore.

I will be there to hold you in times of trial,
I will rejoice when laughter fills your heart,
I will lay down my life that you may prosper,
I will love you, as Christ loves you, with all my heart.

Stand beside me as Christ is our witness,
Of the vows that we make to each other now,
I pledge my love, my compassion, and my faithfulness,
And vow to help you reach our mansion beyond the stars.

With You Beside Me, a Song

You have brought a special meaning to each dawning,
You have made the roses bloom with fragrance sweet,
And though we've traveled a rocky road, His love has kept us,
Safe and secure within the shadow of His throne.

CHORUS

With you beside me, I know we can make it,
Up the stairway that leads to heaven and home,
With your love to enfold and keep me going,
And the light of Christ within to lead us home.

There is no other I would choose to walk beside me,
For with each passing day I love you more,
In your eyes I see the gentleness of Jesus,
And in your life I see the image of my Lord.

There is no doubt that the Lord brought us together,
For in the years that have passed I've seen His grace,
And as we now renew our vows to each other,
I can see the calm assurance on His face.

The Other Man, a Poem

Throughout the years you've often mentioned,
That you suspected there was someone else in my life,
"Another man?" you so often questioned,
But I never answered, only smiled.

Today I feel it's time you knew,
The truth about this situation,
That through all these years that have passed,
Another man has been with me through the duration.

You see, every time my heart was broken,
I'd run into His arms,
And He'd hold me and comfort me,
And give me courage to go on.

And though I loved you when you hurt me,
I did not like you,
And I'd find sanctuary,
In the other man's love.

When He had calmed me and strengthened me,
He always sent me back to you,
And I forgave you, because He asked me to,
Without the love of the other man, I would have walked away years ago.

But with His help I stayed,
To walk beside you, to encourage you,
And because I belong to Him,
I still belong to you.

So on this day, the day we celebrate our marriage vows,
I want you to know that there is another man in my life,
His name is Jesus,
And because of His love for me,
I am still in love with you.

Messenger, a Poem

Dedicated to those who are both spouse and precious caretaker

Lord, in your infinite wisdom,
You have given me a very special assignment,
The one I love most on this earth,
Has a great need for Your love,
A great need for Your tenderness,
A great need for your gentleness and healing;
At times it is not easy,
At times I must call upon You for a greater strength, a greater courage,
To be all my dear one needs me to be;
You are always faithful to supply everything I need and more,
And as I go about my daily tasks,
I find myself looking toward the sky more often,
Looking for a hint of Your precious face looking down at me,
And every day I realize how very thankful I am to You,
For giving me this sweet, precious gift in my life;
Thank You for choosing me to be the one who holds him,
While you heal him,
For in this very special place,
And very special time that You have chosen for me,
I grow and learn and have become closer to You,
Than ever before,
And here I am free to become,
All You intended me to be,
Not in spite of what I must do,
But because of what I have learned of Your love;
Thank You, Lord,
For allowing me to be Your messenger of love,
To my best friend on this earth,
And thank You for bringing this,
Very special human being into my life.

The Call of Christ

Let's be ready to take His "call" and be ready to act as His hands, heart, and arms when that "call" comes.

Jesus gave us the Great Commission before He went back to heaven.

He said, "Go." He told us to go everywhere and teach people about the gospel.

He told us to baptize in the name of the Father, the Son, and the Holy Spirit.

Every Christian has been called into service for the King.

We all have different ways we serve Him and different jobs He has given us to do. One means of service is not greater than the other. Each has equal importance, because it takes all of us, serving in the capacity that He has called us to, to make the entire body complete.

So whether He calls us to vacuum the church, teach Sunday school, serve food to the congregation, minister on the streets to the homeless and hurting, or travel around the country preaching the gospel, the most important thing is that we do our very best at what He has called us to do. That's because it gives Him glory when we do and helps the entire body to function.

He also calls us in many different ways every day. He may call you to bring a hot cup of coffee to a coworker who has his or her leg in a cast, to give a larger tip to a waitress or waiter that's in need, to let someone else have a parking place, to buy a meal for someone who is cold and hungry, to pray for someone who speeds by you on the interstate, or even to forgive … when you are sure it will be impossible for you to do so.

We just must be ready and listening for that "still, small voice," and the unction of the Holy Spirit, so that we may answer His call.

And dear ones, when He does call, I pray that He may never get "a busy signal."

I Will Go, a Poem
Written in tribute to Sister Dollie, a champion of the faith.

There are so many, Lord,
Hopeless souls who need Your love,
Cold and hungry, weary, worn,
They haunt the corners of my mind,
Empty hands, searching hearts,
Haunted eyes of children needing care.

Where shall I begin, Lord?
How much can I, one person, do?
Yes, Lord, I hear, yes, Lord, I will go,
I will take what I have, I will go where You direct,
I will give, give of myself,
And maybe in some small way, I can lift the load of a brother,
Give tenderness to a lost sister; bring a ray of sunshine to a child.

There will be enough,
Somehow there will be enough,
You will provide,
Down from heaven the gifts will come,
And hungry hearts and bellies will be fed,
All I know is that I trust You, Lord.

I will not give up,
Together You and I,
Will touch those we can reach,
Reach those we can touch,
And maybe through it all, souls will be saved,
And devastated lives may be replenished.

I love You, God, I love them too,
It doesn't matter how they look,
How they talk or walk, how they live,
I love them all, because they are Yours,
And I am Yours,
And I will go, Lord,
I will go.

No More Throwaways, a Song

Today it seems that everything is being recycled,
Aluminum, glass, paper, and tin,
We have to conserve and make sure we're not wasting,
So why do we throw away people and leave them to die in sin?

CHORUS

There must be no more throwaway people,
No more left to die,
All of God's children need a chance to fly,
If we care enough about old newspapers,
And walk miles to save a soda can,
Surely we can lend a hand to a brother or sister,
Who's perishing in our own land.

The roads are filled with people who are searching,
Trying to find a reason to press on,
Reach out a hand; give a cup of cool water,
Quench a thirsty soul in the name of the Lord.

SPOKEN
How much longer will God allow the waste to continue?
How many more children, teenagers, and grandparents
Will He allow us to sacrifice?
Can we profess our love for Christ and ignore those who cry for mercy?
When it's all over, someone will have to pay the price,
Will we try to lay it all on Christ?

Wear Not His Name in Vain, a Poem

The day had finally come; the day that the Lord said would arrive,
Seated upon His golden throne, He began to judge my life,
Scenes passed before me of the things I'd said and done,
Happy times, sad times, and then there appeared a shameful one,
I looked upon the face again of a young man I had known,
He had grown up in our church and had always called it home,
That is until he began to run with a wild and crazy crowd,
And I cautioned all my children that his presence was not allowed,
He wore strange clothes and cut his hair in a fashion I did not like,
He began to act different and exchanged a skateboard for his bike,
Then came that night, I remember it well, that he appeared at my door,
And he asked to come inside and talk about the Lord,
My laughter flashed before me, and I winced as I saw my face,
I didn't look much like a disciple of Jesus,
And where was the Savior's grace?
Then I saw his eyes just before he turned away,
And I saw the pity there,
For me? I was shocked! Why he was the one, who couldn't make it here,
Then I looked up into the face of Jesus, and saw the same look in His eyes,
And I knew that my robe had been soiled,
By a heart that had spoken lies,
I had called myself a Christian,
Lord, forgive me for taking Your name in vain,
Forgive me for not really knowing the Savior,
And for causing others pain,
For if we are to wear the name of the Savior, Jesus Christ,
We must truly love others as ourselves,
And as He, lay down our lives,
This young man who came to me for help,
Now stands within heaven's gate,
And I, who could have been the lucky one,
To love him into the kingdom,
Await my promised fate.

Shades of Gray Rap

The Bible is black and white,
Everything you do is sin or it's right,
There's no gray in the middle, do you know what I mean?
There's no way to be just a little between.

God is a holy God,
If you serve Him, then take your head and nod,
He washed away your sin, and made you white as snow,
Now how do you think you can dabble in the flow of the world?

CHORUS
Are you turning to shades of gray?
How is your faith leanin' today?
A little bit of the world is okay?
Turnin' your walk with Jesus into gray, into gray.
Shades of gray!

Now is the time to get right,
Turn off the tube, read your Bible tonight,
You won't find forgiveness in the world you try to please,
You'll find salvation down on your knees.

He's comin' for a people who are holy and pure,
Walkin' in the light, not shades of what we were,
Today is the day to get right,
Come out of the middle and hang with the light.

Don't be turnin' to shades of gray,
Get on your knees and read the word today,
Jesus will show you the way,
Playin' in the world will turn your faith to shades of gray!

I Don't Wanna Play Rap

Fed up with livin' in the world every day,
I picked up my sticks and just walked away,
From the noise of the boys and the girls at play,
The world and its toys couldn't hear me anyway,
I got down on my knees with the Man,
The One with the scars in the palms of His hands,
The One who bled and died for me,
Who laid down His life to set mine free.

CHORUS
I don't wanna play, play the world's silly games today,
Jesus has a better way, walkin' with Jesus is where I'm gonna stay!

I took the remote and I threw it away,
I took the TV out and I sold it today,
I opened the book, the one that's holy,
The one that teaches us to be His solely,
I read the word, turned up the sound,
Of my voice as I spoke the word out loud,
I felt the power of the Spirit rise up in me,
And I began to praise the Man from Galilee!

Get down with the Man with the scars in His hands,
Let Him touch you, let Him love you,
Shake off the world and all of its ploys,
Let the devil have back all his toys,
Step up, step out of the world today,
Stand up, stand out, and let Jesus have His way,
Don't let the lies of the world enslave you,
Hang with the One who straight out made you!

I'm plantin' my feet right here in the word,
In the power of the Spirit, in the light of the Lord,
And to all the people who are hurting today,
The brothers and the sisters are on their way,
And we're not stoppin', we're not droppin',
'Til you are safe with in Him! We're takin' His people back!

Transformed, a Song

When I looked into the mirror today, I couldn't believe my eyes,
When I gazed at the image there, it was in great surprise,
For I realized through trial and pain, a change had taken place,
And when I looked into the mirror today, I saw only Jesus' face.

CHORUS

Less of me, more of Thee,
Holy Spirit inside of me,
Less like me, more like Thee,
That all may see only Jesus, only Jesus.

I have been transformed by His love, into the image of His Son,
Each time I've laid aside my life and died to the flesh like Christ,
Each time I've carried another's load and humbly bowed down low,
Each time I bore the cross of love, I became more like Jesus.

This bruised and battered body, with its nail-scarred hands and feet,
Is the picture of a soldier who has never known defeat,
Being crucified with Jesus, dying in a brother's place,
A life of overcoming, laying all at Jesus' feet.

CHORUS

A Heart That Can Shed Tears, a Song

Oh Lord, I thought I knew how to love You,
I thought I'd loved You for a very long time,
But in truth, my heart was one of rebellion,
And a heart of stone cannot love Jesus Christ.

CHORUS

Precious Lord, give me a heart of understanding,
Melt it down, and teach it how to feel,
For my heart cannot feel the pain of others,
Until it learns to really love You.

The Bible says that those who have a broken heart,
Are the ones who will always find You near,
My heart is willing, now, to be broken down,
To be replaced by a heart that can shed tears.

Who Will Be Guilty? A Song

Love never faileth, the holy Scriptures say,
So why do I treat your children in a self-righteous way,
When I need to love them, out of the terrors of hell,
And freely give them, from the waters of Your well.

CHORUS

Lord, give me a fire that cannot be quenched,
A love for Your children that is truly heaven sent,
A hunger for the Bible and a driving need to pray,
And keep my eyes on Jesus 'til the dawning of that day.

Lord, give me the courage, and dispel all the fear,
Help me to witness and open ears to hear,
If I don't speak of Jesus and my friend then is lost,
I'm not a real friend, and the price too high a cost.

I want to share Jesus; I want to lend a hand,
To souls that are drowning, with their mansions built on sand,
If I keep my silence, and they're lost in the tide,
Who will be guilty when the books are opened wide?

Going Home

Going home is hard for all of us. Our hearts break when a loved one dies, and it can be terrifying if we find ourselves very ill and all control has been taken out of our hands.

When we see a vase of beautiful flowers, we know that we will have that vase long after the flowers have died and been thrown away. It is lasting, but the fresh flowers, no matter how beautiful they are, or how sweet their fragrance, are only temporary.

It is different with us, however. That vase, that vessel that we see, that holds the rose of our spirit was not meant to last forever, but the rose, the very essence of all we are, will never die but will live for all eternity.

So, unlike the fresh-cut flowers in the vase, our vessel is meant to be broken, so that the beautiful rose that has resided within might be released at last to return to the Savior's garden in heaven.

There, each precious rose will never wither, never lose its beautiful color or its wonderful fragrance!

But it will live and grow and shed its precious fragrance throughout heaven for all eternity.

It Is an Awakening, a Poem
For sweet Mary.

It is a hard thing we go through,
To be born out of this body,
And into the kingdom of Christ,
Our vessels have served us well,
And do not want to let go,
Of the presence within,
That cries out for the arms of its Father,
Sometimes we do not seem like ourselves,
Because a part of us
Is already reaching out of us,
And grasping a piece of heaven,
We often cannot remember those close to us,
Because our minds and hearts,
Are fixed on the sweet strains of music,
That we hear faintly echoing through the clouds,
Beckoning to us with its sweetness,
And that sweetness makes it hard to concentrate,
On things that are still bound to earthly realms,
Our earthly mortal being,
Slowly begins to fall asleep,
As our immortal soul begins to awaken,
To the sights and sounds of our true reality,
Our home with our Father,
As we are born into eternity,
We fall asleep to our temporal being,
And then in a moment,
In the twinkling of an eye,
We are born and transformed
Into forever.

I Just Ran on Ahead, a Poem

You know how excited I've always been,
About new things and new adventures,
I've always been one to forge ahead,
And now that I have ventured onward,
To new vistas, new joys, and a new life in heaven,
I want you to know that I'll be waiting,
In our new home just beyond the stars;
Someday, when your work on earth is done,
And Jesus calls for you,
To venture forth as I have done,
I'll be waiting to meet you in our mansion;
I just ran on ahead to get everything ready,
And someday, He'll bring you home to me,
Then all our tomorrows, for all eternity,
Will be happy ones;
Until then, I'll be watching over you,
From just beyond the stars.

Labor of Birth, a Poem

Do not sorrow at my death,
Nor grieve that I am gone,
For laughter is my constant state,
Now that I am at home.

For when I shed the vessel clay,
That kept me from my Lord,
I was born of spirit free,
And carried heavenward.

Rejoice that I no more am bound,
By time, and earth, and space,
But walk the gardens side by side,
With Jesus face to face.

What earth has seen as but an end,
Is far from the real truth,
For it was not death I felt,
But the labor of my birth.

Walk Me Home, Jesus, a Song

You've been with me every day of my life,
Though the road sometimes has been rough,
You've held me in the strength of Your arms,
And surrounded me with Your love,

Someday when the timing is right,
For me to come back to my home,
And the mission You gave me is done,
Jesus, will You please walk me home?

CHORUS

Walk me home, Jesus,
I need my hand in Yours,
Walk me home, Jesus,
To heaven's very doors,
There's no other way for me to get,
Across the crystal sea,
Walk me home, Jesus,
Hand in hand, walk me home.

When I see the bright, shining stars,
Like crystal on a black velvet sea,
I think of You in my home just beyond,
And know that someday, You'll come for me.

Precious Memories

For those precious loved ones who have gone on home to wait for us.

The beauty of their presence and their legacies are still alive and well in our hearts.

We shall be together again someday, and then we shall never again have to part.

Take care of our loved ones, Lord, until we all get home.

There's an Angel, a Song
For Mama

There's an angel gone home to heaven,
And this old earth will never be the same,
But I know she's glad to be back in heaven,
For it was from heaven Mama came.

CHORUS

And the angels ran to meet my mama,
When her feet touched the streets of gold,
And Jesus was there to greet my mama,
And Daddy was there, her to hold.

There's a great jubilation in heaven,
For a daughter of the king has returned,
The feast is laid upon the table,
A snowy gown and golden crown wait for her.

Mama, you are a great beauty,
Arrayed in the robes of royalty,
Standing there with a smile beside Daddy,
What a blessed homecoming I see.

Today Snow Came from Heaven, a Song
For Sonny and his beloved mom
Thank you, Brother Sonny, for naming me Little Orange Shoes

CHORUS

Today it's snowing in New Mexico; the desert wears a gown of white,
Softly it tapped at my window, late in the night,
And I smiled and felt the warmth of love surround me once again,
Like the arms of a mother's love, and the softness of her hand.

When my mother was born, they named her Snow, Nieves in my native tongue,
No sweeter soul was ever born than the one I called my mom,
Much too soon she followed Dad, winged her way to heaven's shore,
Casting off endless cares of earth, her spirit free at last to soar.

And that day Snow came to heaven and entered softly through the gate,
Then settled on the streets of gold, patiently to wait,
Jesus took Snow in His arms and held her oh so tight,
Set a golden crown upon her head, gave her a gown of snowy white.

CHORUS

Yes, today snow was sent from heaven,
To remind me of my mother's love,
Every snowflake is a gentle kiss,
Sent from Mama in heaven above.

My Precious Son, a Poem
For Kathy

My precious son, you have taught me so much,
You cannot speak to me,
I have never heard you say Mama with your voice,
But I have seen my name in a sudden sparkle of knowing in your eyes;
You cannot tell me how you feel, or what you think,
Yet I have felt your love in your labored smile;
You cannot run to me with your legs,
Yet I have seen your heart run to mine,
When you turn to the sound of my voice;
You cannot tell me of the Creator,
And yet I learned of His great love from you;
You, my precious son,
Are my inspiration and my joy,
In your life, mine has been made richer,
And I have learned the most precious lessons of life from you;
I have learned that the measure of a man,
Is not how tall he stands,
Or what great feat society says he has accomplished,
It isn't even in the words he says, or doesn't say;
I've learned that the true measure of a man,
Is found in how much he is loved,
And to me, my son,
You stand ten feet tall!
For I love you with all my heart;
My precious son, I thank God for blessing me,
With such a great teacher and friend,
And although you may not speak with your voice,
I know that He hears every thought,
For I know He cherishes you too,
And someday, when we all go to live in His house,
I will hear your voice, and your laughter, and see you run,
And we will dance together, my son and I;
Until then, we shall let His love grow in us,
And I shall continue thanking Him each and every day,
For His great gift to me, my precious son.

He Loved You Too Much to Let You Stay, a Poem
For a friend whose child went home soon after birth

I watched the rosebud begin to grow,
Carefully assessed its progress each day,
With hopeful heart and watchful eyes,
I found it hard to wait.

For the tiny bud to burst forth in bloom,
That I might smell its fragrance sweet,
That I might touch its petals soft,
And hold it close to me.

Then just as its tiny petals opened,
To let its face turn toward the sun,
I saw a hand reach toward the bloom,
And I cried, "No! Not this one!"

This one is mine; I've watched it grow,
I've tended it every day,
You cannot take my rosebud,
You cannot take it away.

Then deep into His eyes I looked,
Where all of heaven shone,
And I saw what a great and fairer place,
Was prepared for this little rose.

I thought the rosebud was only my own,
And yet, it had belonged to Him,
He too had watched it every day,
His love shining forth from within.

I knew then that He had chosen this little rose,
For the beauty of His own heavenly garden,
And though I missed its fragrance sweet,
I knew no greater honor could be given.

And so, sweet little rose, I love you,
And I'll think of you each day,
But I know you bloom beside His throne,
And He just loved you too much to let you stay.

A Man I Can Look Up To, a Song
Dedicated to my precious brother, Ray

You are my big brother, a godly man to see,
The example of everything a real man should be,
You spent most of your life in uniform; you gave all to keep us free,
A faithful patriot of our country, and a hero to me.

CHORUS

As a little girl I thought you were taller than the trees,
A man who always walked straight and tall and was all I wanted to be,
You are a man who stood,
For all that was good,
And you lived your life with love,
You are a man I can look up to,
My hero and guardian angel from above.

You've always found some good in everyone; you've called so many strangers
friend,
And the American soldiers and veterans are remembered because you
fought to speak for them,
I am so proud to be your little sister, and I cherish each day we share,
You are a man I can look up to, a big brother who's always cared.

And now you've gone to heaven, your mission finally through,
You were called by the Supreme Commander to receive the rewards you're
due,
And as I look up into the sky, I know the soldier has come home,
I can see the man I still look up to standing by God's throne.

CHORUS

Father,

It is my prayer that every person reading this little book will come to know Your glorious love, Your faithfulness, and Your forgiveness. May each one safely find Your pathway home, and may they dwell in the house of the Lord forever.

In the name of Christ Jesus, I thank You for prayer answered.
Amen.

If you have not yet asked Jesus to come into your heart, forgive your sins, and as the Bible says, change you into a brand new creation, now may be the very time that Jesus is calling to you to come into a relationship with Him.

You can pray this little prayer: *"Father, I believe that Jesus is Your only Son and that He died on the cross and shed His blood to cleanse me from all sin. I am sorry for my sins and ask You to forgive me now. Jesus, please come into my heart and be my Lord. This I pray in Jesus' name. Amen."*

If you prayed this prayer, welcome to the family of God!

You will want to find a good church that teaches the truth of God's word, and you will want to think about being baptized and to begin to study the Bible.

If you are inside the walls, you might want to contact your chaplain and share that you have just taken the first step to completely change your life. Your chaplain should be able to help you obtain a Bible if you do not have one. He or she can also advise you of Bible studies and church services available that will help you in your new walk in Christ.

About the Author

Janet Susan Williams submitted her first song lyrics at age ten, and at age sixteen, she was invited to the Nebraska governor's mansion to discuss her work. She has been writing songs, poetry, and short stories since then. Her poetry has been read on radio and television, has been internationally published by Blue Mountain Arts greeting cards (under the pen name Janet Kostelecky Nieto), and has been recognized by three New Mexico state governors. Mrs. Williams is also affectionately known as "Little Orange Shoes," a name that she often uses in ministry. Her songs and poetry reflect on many different aspects of life, but all have a deep focus on the healing and delivering power of the cross of Christ and God's magnificent love. Her greatest desire is to use God's gifts as a means to glorify God and to convey His love, His compassion, His encouragement, and His saving grace to the world around her.